Advance Praise for
The Art of Talking with Your Teenager

Paul Swets' new book coaches parents of teens and pre-teens to win the communication game. He guides parents past the opponents of misunderstanding, frustration, and ineffective listening skills and helps them achieve the goal of a stronger, closer relationship with their teens. When parents win this game, so do their teens!
> — PAT WILLIAMS
> General Manager, Orlando Magic

I was a single mother for eighteen years and am presently an activist in teen pregnancy and HIV prevention. I am convinced that applying the realistic, practical, and uncomplicated basics outlined in Dr. Swets' very timely book can be a lifesaver to both parent and child who are struggling to maintain needed, healthy family relationships in a society that often undermines those very efforts.
> — PATRICIA FUNDERBURK WARE
> Director of Educational Services,
> Americans for a Sound AIDS/HIV
> Policy

The Art of Talking with Your Teenager *should be on the reading list of every concerned parent or youth worker. It demonstrates something I have believed and practiced for many years—listen to your children and they will listen to you!*
> — JACK ECKERD
> founder of Eckerd Drug Stores

Healthy communication is critically important to me and my family. In this book, I've found principles that work in resolving conflicts and sustaining a strong, close relationship with our teenager and five soon-to-be teenagers.
> — DAVID LEESTMA
> astronaut and director of
> NASA Flight Operations

A helpful and straightforward guide to replacing frustrating arguments with constructive conversations.

— WILLIAM KILPATRICK
author of *Why Johnny Can't Tell Right from Wrong*

Offers wise and practical advice on how to listen so teens will talk and talk so teens will listen. In an age of toxic social forces, family disintegration, and exploding youth violence, such guidance is much needed.

— DAVID G. MYERS
author of *The Pursuit of Happiness*

If only every parent of an adolescent child could read this book and apply the wonderful guidance offered by Paul Swets. My husband and I are delighted to have this book to share with our sons as they enter adolescence. It is especially important to me as an excellent resource in my work with adolescent girls through the Best Friends program.

— ELAYNE G. BENNETT
founder and executive director of the Best Friends Foundation

Having seven children has taught us the importance of leading by example. But we can only lead if we know where we are going. This book points the way through the detours and around the roadblocks common in parenting adolescents. It will help parents lead the way in gaining a better understanding to achieve better results.

— DEXTER R. YAGER, SR.
author of *Don't Let Anybody Steal Your Dream*

The Art of Talking with Your Teenager *can help parents restore understanding, strengthen relationships, and welcome their children home.*

— RUTH BELL GRAHAM
author of *Prodigals and Those Who Love Them*

THE ART OF TALKING WITH YOUR TEENAGER

PAUL W. SWETS

ADAMS MEDIA CORPORATION
Holbrook, Massachusetts

For all the parents
who never give up

Published by Adams Media Corporation
260 Center Street, Holbrook, MA 02343

ISBN: 1-55850-478-8

Printed in the United States of America.

J I H G F E D C

Library of Congress Cataloging-in-Publication Data
Swets, Paul W.
    The art of talking with your teenager / Paul W. Swets.
        p.   cm.
    Cover has subtitle: Staying calm in difficult situations, confronting major problems, hearing what your teen is really saying.
    Rev. and updated ed. of: How to talk so your teenager will listen, 1988.
    Includes bibliographical references and index.
    ISBN 1-55850-478-8 (pbk.)
    1. Parent and teenager—United States. 2. Adolescent psychology—United States. 3. Communication—Psychological aspects. I. Swets, Paul W. How to talk so your teenager will listen. II Title.
    HQ755.85.S937 1995
    649'.125—dc20   94-46831
                                                                CIP

SONG LYRICS ON PAGES 57–58: "Cat's in the Cradle," words and music by Sandy and Harry Chapin. Copyright ©1974 by Story Songs, Ltd. All rights reserved. Used by permission. CHART ON PAGE 70: Taken from the book *A Guide to Child-Rearing* by S. Bruce Narramore. Copyright ©1972 by The Zondervan Corporation. Used by permission of Zondervan Publishing House. CHART ON PAGE 122: From *The Art of Talking So That People Will Listen*, Copyright ©1993 by Paul W. Swets. Reprinted by permission of the publisher, Simon & Schuster, Inc.

This book is available at quantity discounts for bulk purchases.
For information, call 1-800-872-5627 (in Massachusetts, 617-767-8100).

Visit our home page at http://www.adamsmedia.com

TABLE OF CONTENTS

FOREWORD

Good communication with my children doesn't come easily for me. Perhaps that's one reason Paul and Jud wrote this book. They had me in mind!

When I say things that cause my son to argue or my daughter to cry, my problem is not that I don't love my children. My problem is that sometimes I don't know how to express my feelings or listen or resolve conflicts in ways that demonstrate that love.

Happily, I'm learning. This book has reduced the strain, the tensions, the hurt feelings, the painful misunderstandings. It has caused my children and me to smile more often.

Talking so teenagers will listen and listening so they will talk takes work. It comes at a high price, but miscommunication costs far more. That's why you will discover passion in this book. It's not just about the mechanics of getting through to our children. Rather, it concerns preventing serious crises and increasing the opportunities for parents, whether married or single, to make a difference in the development of happy, well-rounded, morally sound, and productive teenagers.

My daughter Jessica and I count it a privilege to know the authors firsthand. They live what they write. We know Paul and Jud could not have produced such a book if they had not first proved its power in their relationship.

Jessica is delighted this book is completed. She's counting on Paul and me to make the most of our best communication skills as she travels through the most critical stage of her adolescence.

—Janiece S. S. Swets

ACKNOWLEDGMENTS

Jud and I want to express our special indebtedness and gratitude to the following:

The single and married parents of adolescents who have constantly been on our minds during the writing of this book. Your hopes and fears, your daily frustrations and occasional victories, your desire to be the best parent you can be—you have inspired the thoughts on each page.

The eight hundred-plus teenagers from Ridgeway and Sheffield High Schools in Memphis, Tennessee; Westminster Academy in Fort Lauderdale, Florida; and Fieldstone High School in Germantown, New York; who responded to our survey.

Clinical psychologists Chuck Hannaford, Doug Hart, Rich Luscomb, and Paul Neal for their valuable input and critical review of the manuscript.

Jan Miller and Dean Williamson, my agents at Dupree/Miller & Associates, for conveying their enthusiasm for this project.

Ed Walters of Adams Publishing, who helped me bring this material to a new level of relevance.

My five sisters—Ethelanne, Marcia, Karen, Faith, Mary—who taught me early on about the need to talk so that others will listen and encouraged me in the writing of this book.

My parents who in many ways, perhaps without knowing it, conveyed the five messages I needed to hear as an adolescent.

And finally, Janiece and Jessica, who daily gave Jud and me enough love and support to get us over writer's block and reach our goal.

A PERSONAL INVITATION TO PARENTS

Why should you read about talking with adolescents? The answer is simple. The way we communicate with our children has an astonishing influence over our family's happiness ... or despair. Research shows an unmistakable correlation between the breakdown of communication in the home and major social problems such as drugs and drinking, out-of-wedlock pregnancies, violent crime, and the epidemic of suicide among our children and adolescents.

Most parents are trying their best to raise their children to be happy and healthy adults. A nationwide poll reveals that our greatest concerns include work, money, health, aging, time management, and family issues. Our concerns about the family, however, are right at the top of the list. Making the family work is our number one goal.

Unfortunately, the family isn't working as well as it should. Part of the problem is that parents aren't well-equipped to understand the crazy world of adolescence. Parents often feel they live in a different world than their teenagers. Even with the best of intentions, their attempts at communication often end in misunderstandings, anger, yelling, and emotional distancing. The sad result is that teens often feel cut off from their parents—the very persons who are most significant to them and could make the biggest positive difference in their growth and development.

Neither parents nor teenagers want it this way. Another survey shows that most teens want to be able to talk to their parents about many things. Both want a closer relationship, but both feel unable to bridge the gap.

Can we learn how to get through to our teens more often? Can we develop the communication skills we need to build stronger relationships? Can we create the closeness both we and our teens want, and build a bridge of understanding that will help us stand strong against the storms of the times?

Yes! More consistent, more effective communication with our teens is possible.

In most cases, failures of communication are caused by a limited number of correctable errors. We're saying and doing a *few* things wrong. Anyone can reduce the number of errors they make, and increase the quality of their relationship. *You* can.

You can't control what your teen will say and think. But you can learn to control yourself—what you say and how you say it—and that may be enough to make a meeting of the minds possible.

This book is designed to help you beat the odds against successful communication with your teen. First, we'll review the basic communication skills as they apply to raising a teenager. Most parents feel that their experience raising their children should qualify them as experts on the subject, but parenting adolescents is a whole new ball game.

Next, we'll examine some field-tested techniques for improving the way we communicate, covering topics such as "Earning The Right To Be Heard," "The Art Of Saying 'No'," and "Listening So That Your Teenager Will Talk." These methods for facing the challenges of everyday living may seem simple, but when our children enter their second decade, even commonplace events or conversations can turn out to be difficult. Putting the principles of these chapters into practice will help you reduce misunderstandings, tensions, anger, and hurt feelings.

Finally, we'll apply the skills and insights we've developed to helping our teens handle the new decisions and challenges they face—from developing healthy lifestyles and making wise decisions to resisting destructive or self-destructive tendencies. You'll see that you have choices on how to talk to your teen, even at the most difficult or critical moments. You'll develop game plans that fit your needs—and your teen's—and that really work.

Each chapter includes Action Steps—practical exercises that will help you develop new communication skills, build your confidence, and serve as valuable practice in putting the techniques to use. They'll help you examine your own experience for clues to effective methods, and give you the feedback you need to make the slight adjustments that are the key to success.

One of the most important things this book can give you is insight into the heart and mind of your teenager. When Judson, my son, became an adolescent, I asked him to join me in writing this book. He accepted! On the way to the tennis courts, jogging around the block, or sprawled on the family room floor, he tested each principle and challenged each assumption. We experienced the truth of the proverb, "As iron sharpens iron, so one man sharpens another."

Together we designed a survey to capture the thoughts and feelings of a broad spectrum of junior and senior high school students. Jud's chapter, "Five Messages Teens Want To Hear," is based on over 800 responses to that survey as well as his own reading and thinking. Understanding teenagers is the key to communicating with them, and this section will help you understand what your teenager means by what he or she says or does.

I encourage you to begin the difficult, but always rewarding process of building a stronger relationship with your teenager. Perhaps you are a single parent with a double responsibility. Maybe the barriers to healthy relationships seem to outnumber your mental and emotional resources. You may cry out for some understanding of your own needs and never get it. But no matter how overwhelmed or underappreciated you feel, doing your best in the present will make a difference—for both you and your teen.

Hopefully, this book will give you the support and encouragement you deserve. It will remind you when you do something wrong. It'll encourage you when the going gets tough. And it will always keep you pointed toward your goal—a stronger, closer relationship with your teen.

As you make progress toward this goal, you will experience the benefits of:

- Knowing what your teen thinks and feels instead of having to guess at what's bothering them
- Reducing the tension and frustration level for both you and your teen
- Enjoying more cooperation in family tasks and responsibilities
- Sharing more interests and activities
- Building mutual respect and caring
- Enjoying a more peaceful, relaxed atmosphere in the home

Our opportunity to make a difference as a parent ends too soon. Let's make the most of it!

CHAPTER ONE

A PARENT'S TOUGHEST CHALLENGE

Even if you are on the right track,
you will get run over if you just sit there.

— WILL ROGERS

Success is never final. Failure is never fatal.
It is courage that counts ... Never give up.

— WINSTON CHURCHILL

If you're the parent of an adolescent, you may be facing the parenting challenge of your life. If you feel you're basically on the "right track" with your adolescent, good! I'm sure you've learned a lot in the process, and you can use this book to keep learning. If you think you've had more failures than successes, good! It only shows that you have high standards and that you want the best for your adolescent. In this chapter we'll begin a process that will help you improve both your parenting skills and the quality of your family life. It'll show you how to make the most of your best parenting instincts and aptitudes and keep you going on the right track.

Recently, during lunch with an attorney friend, he lowered his voice and said, "I don't get it. I try to do everything right as a parent. I really care about my son, but when I tell him anything, his eyes glaze over and his mind is a million miles away. I just can't get through to him."

This parent shares the high level of dissatisfaction dominating many American families. Marriage and family counselors report that the inability to communicate—to listen well and to get through to one another—accounts for most of the problems they see. In more than twenty-five years of teaching, counseling, and listening to parents about their relationships with their teenagers, I have found a persistent, almost desperate desire for something better. Here are a few examples.

"When we were newly married, we looked forward to having children. Although there were minor irritations when they were young, no problem compared with the joy of my five-year-old Susan looking up at me and saying, 'I love you, Daddy!' or eight-year-old Trevor saying 'Dad, I think you need a break. Let's go fishing.' Now they're adolescents and I'm a stranger to them."

"We never had any trouble talking with Jane. She would talk with us nonstop about everything that happened in school and who her friends were. But when she became fifteen, she just stopped talking."

"I'm a single parent. When my children were younger, I had to be very creative about discipline, but I always found ways to get them to behave. Now my son is on drugs and my daughter treats me like dirt. What have I done wrong?"

Can you feel the pain in these parents' comments? Perhaps you, too, are in a situation with your teen that gives you grief. Or maybe you're looking for ways to prevent major problems from happening in the future. Whatever your situation, by picking up this book you have started to do something about it. You were probably interested because you care about building or maintaining a strong relationship with your children—a bridge that enables you to reach them, understand them, and touch their hearts.

Teenagers also want this bridge to be strong. Research shows that teens want to talk with their parents about what they feel, who they want to become, and how they can make sense of their lives. Although their peers have enormous influence, at a deeper, more significant level it's often their father and mother whom they turn to for validation and approval. The "Look, Mom! No hands!" of childhood has its counterpart on the junior high school football field and at the high school science exhibit.

In a survey my son and I conducted of over eight hundred junior high school and high school students from different parts of the country, 89 percent said that their greatest concern in the home was the breakdown of communication.

"I wish I could talk to my mother. Sometimes I just want to bounce my ideas off her, but it always ends up with her lecturing me. I know she loves me, but it seems that she can't let me grow up or have any ideas of my own."

"When I talk with my Dad, we don't talk. We yell. I wish he would listen to my point of view. I wish we could discuss things like I can with my coach."

"When things don't go right between my parents and me, the whole family suffers. Everybody is angry. Maybe it's all my fault."

"The way my mom talks to me makes me feel great, like an adult. She respects me and my feelings just as I do hers. On the other hand, my stepdad makes me feel like hitting him, or running away sometimes just to escape his hurting words. I wish he could learn to treat me with respect."

Can we learn to relate in ways that enable us to achieve a stronger, closer relationship with our teens? Yes! There are no easy solutions or simple formulas. But there are several things we can do that will make a significant difference ... beginning now.

The first step will be to develop a better picture of just how you rate as a family communicator. Are you the kind of parent who can talk easily and naturally with your child on nearly every subject? Or do you often find yourself wishing you knew just what went on in your teenager's head, or how to tell them how hurt or upset you are without totally ruining what little communication you share? Many parents have no idea what their communication style is—much less whether it's working or not.

Take a Self-Inventory

What are your strengths and weaknesses as a communicator? You may have a vague idea of some new directions in which you would like to go, but you really "can't get there from here" if you don't know where "here" is.

The following inventory can help determine where you are now in your skill development and where you may need to make improvements. Adopt the attitude that you have nothing to lose and perhaps a great deal to gain by rating these statements as truthfully as possible. For each statement, circle the number that best represents how often the statement is true (1 = seldom, 2 = sometimes, 3 = often, 4 = usually).

1 2 3 4	1. My teenager listens to what I say.
1 2 3 4	2. When communication breaks down, I adjust what I say and how I say it and try again.
1 2 3 4	3. When I talk with my teen, I keep in mind the developmental characteristics of adolescence.
1 2 3 4	4. I ask questions and make statements that help my teen through the various areas of adolescent development.
1 2 3 4	5. I work at earning the right to be heard.
1 2 3 4	6. In emotional situations, I think about the consequences of my words before I speak.
1 2 3 4	7. I listen to my teen at least as much as I talk.
1 2 3 4	8. My teen talks to me about his or her feelings and problems.
1 2 3 4	9. When communication breaks down, I understand why.
1 2 3 4	10. I repair communication breakdowns.
1 2 3 4	11. I respond effectively when my teen is angry.
1 2 3 4	12. I defend myself verbally against attacks in a way that promotes understanding.
1 2 3 4	13. When necessary, I confront and say no to my teen without losing my temper.
1 2 3 4	14. I discipline my teen in a way that wins respect.
1 2 3 4	15. I am aware of how my temperament influences communication with my teen.
1 2 3 4	16. In matters of discipline, I give my teen a consistent message.
1 2 3 4	17. I am conscious of the major problems teenagers face.
1 2 3 4	18. I help my teen figure out ways to meet these problems successfully.
1 2 3 4	19. When conflict arises, I follow a clear plan for trying to resolve it.
1 2 3 4	20. In the midst of a conflict, I state my views calmly.
1 2 3 4	21. I talk to my teen about life's major decisions.
1 2 3 4	22. I model the kinds of choices I want my teen to make.
1 2 3 4	23. I know the messages my teen wants to hear from me as a parent.
1 2 3 4	24. I communicate these messages to my teen.

How did you do? Would you like to find out? Determine your score by adding each of the numbers you circled; then check your total points with the following guide:

92-96 Super—In fact, your score might be "incredible." Would your teen rate you approximately the same on each of these items? If so, you need not read on. Give this book to a friend.

78-91 Good—You are on track. You have a grasp of some basic caring communication skills. Keep going and refine them for even greater success.

50-77 Fair—You are missing some of the joy of communication with your teen. If you want to make some changes and experience success, you can. Remember that even small changes can produce great gains. Read each chapter carefully and take time to do the Action Steps. Look for parenting seminars in your area that will help to reinforce what you are learning. Talk with a counselor, pastor, or rabbi for support and direction.

24-49 Poor—Are you being too hard on yourself? Keep in mind that you might not be responsible for how your teen responds to you. If communication is ineffective, it might not be your fault. You are responsible for yourself and what you can control. It is possible that you are in a seriously dysfunctional relationship. If so, seek professional help. You may need emotional support or clinical counseling to help improve your relationship with your teen.

Become an Expert on Your Teen

The goal of this test is not to cause you to doubt yourself or make you feel insecure about your ability as a parent. It's simply to show you how to apply what you already know about parenting to communicating with your teenager.

When our children are young, we know the rules that govern talking and listening reasonably well. After all, we make the rules! And we manage quite well, perhaps—until adolescence.

Adolescence represents a major paradigm shift—a fresh set of rules fueled by new desires, a deeper sense of self, a higher level of internal turbulence and confusion, and a driving desire for independence from authority and acceptance by their peers. The result is a whole new pattern of relating that most parents find confusing. (We'll take a closer look at the nature of adolescence in chapter 2.)

Be Trained, Not Blamed

Most of us will need to learn some new skills to cope with the communication challenges we'll face while raising a teenager. We haven't been trained in how to respond to strong emotions, how to resolve conflicts, how to employ active listening techniques, or how to talk with our children so that they will want to talk to us. Our lack of training often results in communication breakdowns, for which we often blame ourselves as well as our children.

This blaming depresses and demotivates. It's futile. Proper training will help us learn what to avoid, what to aim for, and how to make the changes necessary to reach our parenting goals.

One company discovered that by training employees in listening skills, they could decrease communication errors and save millions of dollars. Research showed that those who had been trained in listening techniques became more highly motivated, made fewer mistakes, and enjoyed their work more than those who did not receive the training.

This book makes the benefits of the same kind of training available to you. As you apply the communication principles outlined in each chapter, you will become a trained expert on communicating with your children.

The Principles of Caring Communication

The key to improving our relationship with our teens is to learn new ways of listening and talking. The old ways are marked by habit. They're comfortable, predictable, easy. We use the same patterns not because they work, but simply because we have used them before. We employ them without thinking; they may even be the same patterns our parents used with us. Unfortunately, upon closer examination these habits may prove to be ineffective or even destructive. Often, the result is not dialogue but *duologue*— two people talking but not connecting.

The alternative is learning how to practice "caring communication." Caring communication involves opening your heart and mind to the heart and mind of your teenager. It is driven not by habit but by three internal principles or motivating forces that can form the basis for the way we listen and talk with our teenagers.

The first principle is _commitment_. If we care about building a stronger, closer relationship with our teenagers, we will need to commit to taking the necessary steps to reach that goal. Changing deep-seated habits can take time, and our commitment will keep us going even when we don't seem to be making progress. It enables us to develop insights and put them to work in a way that shows our care and concern. When we commit ourselves to becoming caring communicators, we pledge to our teenager that we'll talk and listen to them to the best of our ability. When we fail (we all do at times), this commitment will compel us to adjust, try again, and eventually succeed.

The second principle is _empathy_. Empathy is the ability to tune into our teen's feelings. When we empathize, we try to look at events at home or school from their point of view as well as our own. If our teens sense that we do not really understand or care about what they are saying, they'll stop listening. But when it is clear that we're doing our best to empathize with how they feel, we'll probably get a hearing—even though our conversational skills may not be the greatest. Empathy helps us not only to view life as our teens view it but also to see ourselves the way they see us ... and make the necessary corrections.

The third principle is _firmness_. Caring communication is not soft or weak. It's firm because it cares. It keeps us from giving in to our own emotional frustrations, from saying things to our teens that we will regret; it also allows us to resist becoming victims of our teens' verbal abuse or manipulation techniques. Firmness is the resolve to steer a path through the obstacles in order to strengthen the relationship.

Caring communication characterized by commitment, empathy, and firmness is an art: a creative blend of insights and skills, a harmony of mind and heart that can produce a deeply satisfying level of understanding. Like any work of art, it doesn't come easily.

Determine Your Communication Goals

Setting goals can help us to focus our minds and hearts on what is important to us and to set clear directions for the changes we need to make. Goals can also motivate us to action. Here are some examples that keep me on target when I talk with my children. My goals are to:

• Think before I speak
• Listen without interrupting

- Avoid a judgmental tone of voice
- Speak calmly without raising my voice
- Ask questions that promote interesting conversation
- Talk to my teen the way I want my teen to talk to me

If our goal is to encourage but our habit is to berate, our goal can help us to develop a new mindset, a more positive way of responding. We might even want to measure how close we are to our goals by recording, for example, the ratio of compliments to criticisms we give within a certain time period. We can actually count or quantify our progress. Communication goals help us know what adjustments are necessary and how to go about making them. They can set our minds on a clear track and focus our attention on our target.

Build a Positive Perspective

What characteristics does the term "teenager" bring to your mind? Forgetful? Arrogant? Rude? Irresponsible? Insensitive? Scatterbrained? Unpredictable? Selfish? Perhaps teens are all of these at various times, but they can also be delightful.

Teenagers can feel deeply the pain or joy of others. They can be humorous, spontaneous, creative, caring, spunky, thoughtful, and fun-loving. At times they may be mature beyond their years, yet youthful enough to dream and to reach for the stars. Being with them keeps us fresh and in tune with the future.

I remember that when our children, Judson and Jessica, were infants, I thought of them as bundles of energy eager to be released, as artistic masterpieces in the process of formation. Consequently, I treated them with great care and respect. When they became adolescents, I realized that my images of them still color what I say and how I say it.

These images have played an important role in shaping their self-images. If I think of my children as irresponsible, I will convey that impression. If I think of them as masterpieces in the process of formation, I am more apt to communicate my support. Since teens are vulnerable and impressionable as they begin the process of forming their own identity, how we think of them and what we tell them they are could have strong influences on what they will become.

The parent's performance as a role model is also crucial. When teens show us their worst selves, we can bring out the best in them by showing them our best selves. If we can talk skillfully and listen intently to them, we create opportunities to build respect, to bridge troubled waters. Of course, the bridge cannot be built in a day. It takes time, patience, persistence, commitment, skill, and a whole lot of love. But isn't that what parenting is all about?

We need to develop a long-range perspective that reaches beyond our momentary frustrations—a view that affirms: "We are family. We are in this together. We are for our teens, not against them." The real obstacles to good communication, for both parents and teens, are negative habits, time pressures, frustrations, self-preoccupations, distractions, past failures, and feelings of hopelessness. In the battle for understanding in the home, our perspective must be that we're going against the odds to succeed as a family. We have to believe it and show it so that our teens see it and are won over by our commitment.

In my counseling I have seen parents and teens completely frustrated with the other. Where there was a desire, even a one-sided one, for healing, coupled with a will to build a strong relationship, frustration eventually gave way to gratitude that they had never given up the struggle for harmony.

Choose Your Words Carefully

When we keep our goals in mind during our conversations, we will choose our words accordingly. Without goals, our choice of words is left to whim, to the feelings of the moment. The word choices below are simple, but the difference our choices produce in terms of attitude and relationship over a period of time can be profound.

Daughter: Do you know where my shoes are?

Choice 1
Parent: You never put them away. That's why you are always losing them!
Daughter: Oh yeah? Why are you always losing your keys?

Choice 2
Parent: I believe you left them by the blue chair.
Daughter: Thanks, Mom.

In choice 1 the parent reacts to the daughter's question with a judgmental statement, attempts to correct a behavior, and generates a controversy. In choice 2 the parent responds without judgment and generates gratitude. The word choices we make in conversation determine the quality and depth of our relationships. Most importantly, they are completely within our control.

Teenagers detect when we are frustrated or angry, but they cannot easily distinguish between our dislike of their behavior and our dislike of them. Sometimes we do not make that distinction, either. They pick up clues not only from our word selection but from our actions, our facial expressions, and our tone of voice. Even though we may deeply love our children, they focus more on our harsh tones or expressions of anger.

Make Slight Adjustments

What's a parent to do when his or her best efforts go nowhere? Take a ten-year time out? Give up? As much as we might like to do so, our best strategy is to make some guided adjustments.

Sometimes these adjustments are on the order of a heart transplant—a cleansing of the soul, a spiritual healing and renewal from the inside out. If you sense you need this kind of adjustment, I urge you to go to your pastor or counselor to get the help you need.

In most cases, our communication patterns require only slight adjustments. Major changes can feel overwhelming; slight adjustments in what we say and how we say it are often more manageable. Bear in mind that even small differences in tone of voice, choice of words, facial expression, or the way we listen can alter our teens' views of us and their responses to us.

A while back, NASA invited my family to watch the launch and landing of the space shuttle in which my cousin, David Leestma, was a crew member. After 133 orbits and 4.3 million miles of travel, it was fascinating to see the 200,000-pound shuttle land precisely on target. The key to this success? Slight adjustments made regularly and deliberately throughout the course of the mission. The way you interact with your teen can also benefit from slight adjustments to stay on target.

Draw upon Your Memory Bank

One valuable resource parents often overlook is their memory of their own adolescence. As you begin to work on your rela-

tionship with your teenager, reflecting on your adolescent attitudes and feelings may help you enormously. Can you remember
some of the struggles you endured socially, physically, and emotionally? Can you recall what your parents said to you that helped,
and what hurt? Can you think of some of the mistakes you vowed
never to make when you became a parent?

You and I have a whole reservoir of important information
buried in our subconscious minds. Out of these "memory banks,"
we can remember how we felt as teens when adults talked to us
with respect, or yelled at us in disgust, or asked us how we felt
about some matter, or complimented us on a job well done.
Almost every idea or suggestion in this book could benefit from
some reflection on your own experience as a teenager. That recall,
combined with your new insights and fresh skills, will help you
choose what kinds of adjustments to make.

The Art of Caring Communication

Author and speech expert Dorothy Sarnoff tells an old and
charming story of a little girl who watched a sculptor as he started work on a fresh block of marble. Some weeks later, the child
returned and saw that a lion was taking shape. Astonished, the little girl tilted her head to one side and asked, "Did you know all
the time that there was a lion inside?"[1]

I believe there is a better self inside each of us that can make
a positive difference in the way we communicate with our
teenagers. How will we find it? We'll chisel away every part of our
family relationship that doesn't belong. The principles of caring
communication, in practice, will act like a hammer and chisel.
They will help you discover the masterpiece of art you and your
teen really are deep inside.

Action Steps for Meeting the Challenge of Caring Communication

Each chapter ends with exercises to help you apply the information you have just learned to your situation, and to take positive control of your communication behavior. When you act on an
idea, you make it your own, and it becomes easier to apply.

• *Identify some obstacles you and your teen have experienced
that interfere with good communication—time pressures, fatigue,*

TV, work schedules, and so on. Make a short list and share it with your teenager to see whether he or she agrees with you. Make a second list of actions you can take to begin to eliminate or get past the obstacles you can control.

• *Since motives are the backbone of any commitment, make a list of all the benefits you would receive from better communication with your teenager.* Post it in a prominent place where you'll be reminded of the benefits everyday.

• *Go back to the self-inventory at the beginning of the chapter and make a list of the communication skills on which you scored poorly—the skills you want to improve.* Focus on one of these skills and write a clear, concrete communication goal related to it. For example, "My goal is to learn a clear plan for conflict resolution" or "My goal is to listen to my teen in such a way that he will enjoy talking to me." Your goal may seem like a small step, but it can have a very significant impact on the quality of your relationship with your teen.

• *Next, ask your teen to rate you (and perhaps himself/herself) on the self-inventory.* Listen carefully to the feedback you get without arguing with the results or trying to defend yourself. How does your teen's evaluation of your communication ability differ from your own? Were there any surprises in their feedback? Is there any way you could test or quantify these differences?

CHAPTER TWO

WHAT MAKES YOUR TEENAGER TICK?

*Dad, you've got to remember that I'm just a kid. It's hard for me
to remember everything. I'll grow out of this. It just takes time.*

— JUD SWETS AT AGE 12

*Young people need a sense of "growing," of being
in a process of transition.*

— DAVID ELKIND[1]

Take your average, well-adjusted healthy kid ... sensible,
coordinated, talkative. He even talks to his parents and
brothers and sisters. He appears as comfortable around
peers as with adults. He's no more concerned about his appearance than a bulldog. His focus is outward—parents, other children, grandparents, aunts and uncles.

Then, almost overnight, his body mounts a revolution. Limbs
elongate and no longer inform each other what they're doing. His
face gets fuzzy, his voice plays humiliating tricks on him, and he
assumes everyone in the world is staring at him. His parents wonder, "Is this really the same kid we potty trained?" And the kid
questions himself—"What's happening? Everything seems different! My name's the same, but who am I?"

Adolescence! As confusing as your VCR, and just as resistant
to programming. No longer children, adolescents are not yet
adults. They are normal human beings in transition. Changes
occur too fast for us to capture. One moment they act like children, the next like adults, then somewhere in between. If we want
to gain a realistic view of them, we need to accept some times of

inconsistency and misunderstanding as normal. And we need patience, for this growing-up process "just takes time."

This chapter presents an overview of the basic changes that happen to almost every child during adolescence. It also presents some very basic communication strategies related to each of these areas of change. Be sure to check out the suggestions in each section—at least a few should prove helpful in your specific situation.

As you read this chapter, compare the traits and trends we look at to those of your teenager, as well as to your own experience of adolescence. You will find some similarities and, of course, some differences. The more you recall of your own adolescent experience, the more you'll understand what your teenager is thinking and feeling. And the more of these new insights you discover, the better your chances of really connecting with your teen.

What Is an Adolescent?

No couple embraces and says, "Let's have an adolescent!" If that were part of the process, there might be a lot fewer of us! Fortunately, we have had several years to prepare for the risk and excitement of parenting adolescents. Yet many parents tell me that they don't feel ready. They have discovered that the difference between raising children and raising adolescents is more than age; it's a new ball game in which the old rules don't apply and the new goal lines are uncertain.

What is adolescence? It's a time of transition roughly equivalent to the teenage years, but often extending beyond them in both directions. I'll define adolescence as the period between the onset of puberty (sexual maturation) and the attainment of full adulthood (when one is self-supporting and legally responsible for one's actions). It is a time of major development physically, socially, mentally, emotionally, morally, and spiritually. It is that dramatic passage from one stage to another in which nearly every aspect of our teens' lives turns new, fascinating, and confounding—to both us and to them.

Over the last hundred years, the duration of adolescence has lengthened. Children have become sexually active earlier in life, and the age at which they're able to support themselves has been postponed, relatively speaking. This prolonged state of change often produces turbulent emotions and conflicting messages. Adolescents want independence, but they usually can't afford it.

They want to risk the dangers of an adult world, but they also want the security of being able to come home. They may be ready for marriage sexually, but they are not ready financially. While their bodies say "Go!" their bank accounts say "No!"

This waiting has a positive side. Most psychologists agree that the primary task of adolescence is the formation of an identity—but that it takes time. Psychologist Erik H. Erikson even proposed "a moratorium on adulthood"[2] that would have provided young people with an extended period of time in which to develop their identity as adults. Ideally, this delay of adulthood can provide teens with time to explore, to laugh, to make mistakes, to start over again, to learn what life is about.

Yet in recent years the "moratorium on adulthood" is in danger of vanishing as a result of the increased stress our society places on our children during their teenage years.

Today's teens face an unprecedented level of social stresses ranging from increased competition for jobs and in school to pervasive violence to easy access to drugs and alcohol to the influence of media that emphasize material achievement and focuses on social aberrations.

Psychologist David Elkind explains that today's social pressures place adult demands on teenagers without giving them adequate tools to respond with, tools such as tested values and examined experience. Without an ethical framework or the experience necessary for coping with adult stress, more and more teens resort to self-destructive methods of coping: drug and alcohol abuse, crime, psychological withdrawal, and even suicide.[3]

If adolescence is to be a reasonably happy and healthy period of transition, teenagers need time to grow, to learn who they are and who they can become. They need adequate time to discover their best selves without the undue pressure of coping with premature adulthood.

What Do We Need to Do?

Caring communication that is committed, empathetic, and firm can significantly reduce these adolescent stresses by offering clear direction when it's needed most. In fact, adolescence offers parents a second chance, a new window of opportunity in which we can influence how our child turns out as an adult.

One father laughed, "When my children reach puberty and start dating, the only thing I'll say to my son is 'Good luck!' and to my daughter, 'Don't get hurt!'"

How absurd! Don't buy the myth that a parent's task is over when his children become teenagers. If we truly love our children, we must take advantage of this period of change and exert whatever positive influence we can.

Like wet clay, teens are still malleable. They are breaking out of their childhood molds and entering a new and qualitatively different realm of thinking, feeling, and acting. It is confusing but exciting. Teenagers sense that they need their parents' knowledge and support to survive. If we exercise caring communication skills, we'll have many opportunities to demonstrate to our teens that we can help share their burden—and some adventures as well.

Remember the embarrassment, the awkward moments, the times of hilarity as well as agony you experienced as a teenager? Again, try to put yourself in your teen's shoes as you consider the changes they're going through. You'll understand your teenager better if you can draw on your memory of your own phases of adolescent development.

Physical Development

During the teenage years, sexual characteristics, voice quality, body shape, coordination, appetite, weight, and height all begin to change dramatically. Since personal identity is strongly related to physical appearance, some teenagers experience what psychologist Erik Erikson calls "identity confusion." They may not be sure who they are or who they want to be from one day to the next. The mood swings related to their hormonal changes are often dramatic. And teens are extremely sensitive about these physical changes. A facial blemish can ruin a whole month of compliments. Sometimes the growth process makes teens feel more tired than adults and decreases their ability to respond effectively to their frustrations and tensions. At other times, their energy seems boundless.

It's not easy to talk with adolescents about physical concerns, especially sex. It's awkward for them and for us. But they worry a lot about their bodies, their rate of development, how they compare with their peers, and whether or not they are "normal." They need us to be available to answer their questions.

When talking to your teenager about physical concerns:

• *Be "askable."* Encourage questions about sex and hygiene. If your daughter asks you about birth-control pills, don't overreact by quizzing her on why she wants to know or implying that she is sexually active. An "askable" parent listens carefully and answers briefly.

• *Be reassuring.* If a daughter's first menstruation catches her (and you) unexpectedly and she panics, let her express her fear and reassure her with accurate information and a positive attitude. Help her to view it as a marvel, something to celebrate, a rite of passage. When your son's acne erupts, assure him that it is most often temporary and treatable.

• *Be informative.* Prepare yourself to provide accurate information and clear values regarding sex. Give them a good book on sexual development to supplement what you tell them. (See the Resources section in the back of the book for suggestions.) Help them learn to view the sexual relationship as a positive and beautiful experience within marriage.

• *Be sensitive.* Never joke about physical characteristics such as height and weight. Psychologist Bruce Narramore writes in *Adolescence Is Not an Illness*, "Some parents attempt to motivate their children through sarcasm or ridicule. They believe teasing or pressuring teens about excess weight or untidiness will force positive changes. But these pressure tactics only create resentment and strong resistance."[4]

If your son thinks his growth spurt will make him a giant, patiently explain that it's normal and will level off. If your daughter is overweight, ask her how you can help her. Would it help to go on a diet together?

• *Be positive about their physical health and appearance.* Talk about the payoffs of being fit. It is a mistake to shower our teens with attention, affection, and time only when they are not feeling well. The message we need to convey to our daughters is that their period is not the end of the world. We need to help our sons realize that scrapes and bruises are no big deal.

• *Emphasize getting well.* To a teenager, braving aches and pains without drawing undue attention to them is a major accomplishment. Health is something to celebrate; a goal worth achieving. As with most everything in parenting, a positive attitude about physical health is caught, not taught. But especially with young adolescents, the "catching" can be reinforced with comments like these:

"I appreciate the fact that you exercise. I can see the results in your muscle tone."

"The way you restrained your desire for sweets and ate a balanced meal today shows a lot of self-discipline. I'm proud of you."

"Your cold is over already. It's amazing how quickly your body recovered."

"I know you didn't feel well today, but you went to school anyway. The way you handled the discomfort impressed me."

Social Development

Do you remember the intensity of your social alliances during adolescence? Although parents still have a great deal of influence, what peers think matters. Teens listen intently to whatever they sense will affect their social relationships. To some degree they are self-centered, for adolescents spend a great amount of energy trying to understand themselves and be accepted by their social environment.

Teens often give the impression that the whole world revolves around them, and they seem surprised when others don't recognize this fact. I remember that as a teen I taped a card to my mirror which read, "It's monotonous to be great without anyone noticing it." My son has the following cartoon above his desk.[5]

One morning my wife said, "Jud, I love you." He responded, "I don't blame you." We decided that we liked that response, because it suggested a strong ego that would be better able to cushion the painful social experiences that often accompany adolescence.

Some social learning is painful. In fact, according to David Elkind, teens often face social changes and conditions that are entirely unexpected and for which they are unprepared. He writes:

"In many respects moving from the culture of childhood to the culture of adolescence is like moving from one society to another; and the change in behavior and conduct the adolescent encounters can lead to a form of shock—peer shock."[6]

Elkind describes three forms of peer shock. First, the shock of exclusion. In childhood, friendships are often determined by who lives nearby. Among teenagers, however, group membership is usually determined by fads, clubs, and cliques. It is a painful experience to feel on the "outside," not to be invited to a party, or worse, to throw a party and have no one come.

Second, the shock of betrayal. Children build friendships based on mutual trust and loyalty. During adolescence, relationships become more complex. Teens may find that they have been used or manipulated by another "friend" to gain some advantage for that person. This pattern occurs when teenagers are led on by members of the opposite sex. A boy may profess love and devotion to a girl in order to take advantage of her sexually and later tell his friends that she is a "tramp." In experiences of exploitation, teenagers become painfully aware of the shock of misplaced trust and betrayed loyalty.

Third, the shock of disillusionment. Children normally accept their friends pretty much as they are, warts and all. But with puberty, they begin to idealize each other. Boys and girls who may not have noticed each other as children now find the opposite sex interesting to look at and be around. Especially in romantic relationships, teenagers imagine the other person to be more than he or she is. The person on whom they have a "crush" seems perfect in every way. These crushes don't last long, because the reality of the human being soon sets in; they are shocked to find flaws in appearance, character, or values, or personal habits that irritate.

When social shocks are combined with the other stresses of adolescence, teenagers face a complex array of pressures and of new tasks to be learned. They need parents who can serve as buffers and guides when needed.

When talking to your teenager about social concerns:

• *Communicate tactfully.* This means that we listen when our teens are willing to talk and ask questions or make statements that help them make wise decisions regarding social relationships. For example, you could say:

> "I like it that Aaron talks with you so easily and seems to have a great sense of humor."
>
> "How would you describe a true friend?"
>
> "I still remember a friend I had in high school. He was easy to talk to. He always seemed to be there when I needed him. I could trust him."
>
> "It can be a painful experience when 'friends' let you down."

The goal is to keep the lines of communication open so that our teens feel they can come to us at any time with their questions or concerns.

• _Be patient._ Although solutions to our teens' social problems may be readily apparent to us, we need to allow them time to grasp the complexity of their problems and learn how to solve them.

• _Stay objective._ We need to be careful what we say about their friends. Because our teens' friends are so much a part of their lives, our teens may view any verbal attack on their friends as an attack on them. If we disapprove of their friends, we need to have good reasons and remain as objective as possible in presenting them. (This means, for instance, avoiding labeling and unfair criticism.)

• _Encourage healthy social exposure._ We can volunteer to entertain our teens' friends at our homes and support supervised group activities, especially for young teens. This will help to broaden their social skills and prepare them for formal dating when they are older.

• _Clarify your expectations._ We will need to initiate some principles and limits about dating and curfew. Maintain a firm but positive attitude about this side of adolescent experience. Take the time to explain limits. We will get along better and exert more influence if our teens get the impression that we are for them, not against them.

• _Model resistance to peer pressure._ We face it too, don't we? At her ninety-third birthday party, one grand woman stated that "the best thing about being over ninety is that you outgrow peer pressure!" Until that time comes for us, we all face the pressure to conform. We can help our teens by our own example (choosing directions we want to take rather than letting ourselves be pressured into something against our better judgment) and by building our teens' confidence in their right to assert themselves when their values run counter to the crowd.

Mental Development

Adolescents begin to think at a new level. In ancient times a child of six or seven was thought to have entered the age of reason, for at that age children begin to use logic. Psychologist Jean Piaget claimed that a second stage of reasoning ability appeared during adolescence. He called this new capability "formal operations"—the ability to deal with possibilities, to think abstractly, to enjoy simile and metaphor, satire and parody.

My wife Janiece and I recognized Jud's new level of thinking in early adolescence. He began to argue, debate, negotiate, and test ideas. We learned that when Jud took the opposite side on any point of discussion, he was not necessarily trying to put us down, make us feel bad, or reject our ideas. He was simply trying to shape his own mental identity or exercise his new thinking capacity. One night during our evening meal, he asked, "What would happen to the rotation of the earth if all the people on the earth began walking in the same direction at the same time?" Then, after a minute of silence, he said, "Dad, you haven't answered my question." I replied, "I'm still trying to imagine it!"

When talking to your teenagers about mental concerns:

• *Encourage their mental development.* Listening to our teens' ideas does not necessarily mean that we agree with them, but it conveys the message that we think their ideas are important. That encourages them to continue talking and thinking. In the process, they often sort out spurious ideas themselves and come to a clearer understanding of what really is important to them.

• *Ask thought questions.* Keep in mind the three conditions or 3 C's of asking good questions: Cues that our teens are willing to talk, a Context that is informal, such as when we are doing something or going somewhere together, and Content that is upbeat rather than heavy.

• *Talk as a friend.* Talk about ideas and feelings that are important to you, much as you would with your friends. Work toward a mutual dialogue that is honest and reflective. One sixteen-year-old girl in our survey wrote:

"I am able to talk with my parents openly about almost anything. My mom is so terrific because she manages to see my side of the situation even when she doesn't agree with me. When she's wrong, she admits it. When she's right, she takes the time to explain why."

• *Allow harmless overstatements.* A teen's thinking is still pretty much in flux. Refrain from reacting to rash statements or a know-it-all tone of voice. It takes time, experience, and education to realize how much one really doesn't know. When my son says that my political views are hopelessly out of date, there is no need for me to get angry or defensive. I remember the idealism of youth and that, when I said such things as a teen, I wanted to be taken seriously. So I respond something like this:

"Son, you make some very good points. I admit that I certainly don't know all that I would like to know. Perhaps my views will change someday ... and maybe yours will too. (Smile) But at this point in my life, this is how I view the situation."

Emotional Development

At times we feel teenagers are on an emotional roller coaster—one moment riding high on a burst of confidence, optimism, and fun-loving play, and the next plummeting to the depths of insecurity, pessimism, and depression. While to us these ups and downs may be senseless, to our teens they are real, even though they may not be able to give us "reasons" for what they feel.

When a teenager explodes saying, "You don't understand!" she is probably right. It may be because our teens don't know the words to describe a feeling and we aren't very good at guessing. We could say, "No, I don't understand ... but I want to and I'm willing to listen until I do understand." Difficult as it is, one of the tasks of understanding adolescents is to discover the reasons of their hearts, to learn what our teens are feeling and why. This helps them gain control over their fluctuating moods and makes them better able to express their feelings.

It ought to be clear to us, perhaps painfully so, that we can't expect our teens to express their feelings better than our own day-to-day example. In chapter 7 we will deal with how to keep your cool when emotions explode. For now, keep in mind that it takes time to learn how to express emotions in a healthy way. It works best in an environment that allows room for differences in temperament (see chapter 9) and also for fresh starts. Our part in teaching our teens emotional control is to talk in ways that represent positive expressions of a wide range of emotions.

When talking to your teenager about emotional concerns

• *Model healthy expressions of feeling.* When we identify our own feelings as accurately and exactly as we can, our teens will learn the vocabulary of feelings. We can also show them how to exercise control as we talk about our own struggles.

> *"When the boss makes me stay overtime at work, I feel very frustrated. It's hard for me to know how to express my feeling in a way that he will understand and that doesn't get me fired."*

> *"When you don't come home at the time we agreed upon, I feel very concerned about your safety. On top of that I feel angry because I assume you probably forgot to call me."*

• *Don't minimize their feelings.* "Cheer up—that's nothing to get upset about" is not helpful, because the teen, who is already distressed, is challenged to defend why the feeling is as strong as it is. This makes the teen think the adult is insensitive, and further communication is likely to be cut off.

• *Don't overreact to emotional lows or highs.* Adolescents need freedom and time to gain emotional balance. Learning to feel deeply and strongly is a significant part of being a fully functioning human being.

If our teens can learn to express feelings in a healthy manner and avoid the really damaging side of emotions (the release of feelings in words or actions that hurt another person), they will have accomplished one of the significant tasks of adolescence.

• *Work on your sense of humor.* Our family loves to laugh about everyday foibles, like what our dog Nellie did the first time we took her to the vet or how I almost spilled a glass of ice water in the lap of Jud's girlfriend the first time we met her. Joining in the hilarity can heighten our teens' sense that we appreciate them. It provides ballast for the turbulent times.

• *Celebrate their achievements.* Unfortunately, sometimes we empathize better with defeats than victories. But times of exuberance and optimism need to be reinforced and shared as much as possible. I will never forget the thrill of hearing Jud's campaign speech when he ran for president of his senior class ... and he won't forget that we were there to experience the excitement with him. That night we went out for dinner to celebrate his victory. One man leaned over and said, "You must be very proud of your son." I replied, "Yes, I am. But I would be just as proud of him if he had not won." I hope Jud won't forget that either.

Moral/Spiritual Development

In healthy families, parents are not afraid to talk about their values and faith with their children. Dolores Curran, in *Traits of a Healthy Family*, writes that in a survey of 551 professionals who ranked a list of 56 possible characteristics of a healthy family, the trait "teaches a sense of right and wrong" was ranked seventh and "a shared religious core" was ranked tenth.[7]

In spite of the importance of these two traits, educators and clinical psychologists report that some children grow up in a moral and spiritual vacuum. When parents' moral codes and beliefs are a confusing blend of the ten commandments, social custom, and self interest, it can adversely affect the moral development of their teenagers. Psychologist David Elkind writes:

> *Teenagers need a clearly defined value system against which to test other values and discover their own. But when the important adults in their lives don't know what their own values are and are not sure what is right and what is wrong, what is good and what is bad, the teenagers' task is even more difficult.[8]*

Elkind indicates that ambivalence on the part of the parent is likely to be interpreted as license by the teenager. When a parent says "I don't know what's right," the teenager hears "I don't care what you do."

The alternative to ambivalence is not dogmatic rigidity but a clear commitment to a system of values that we believe in and that will promote healthy moral development in our teens.

Dr. Robert Coles, teacher, research psychiatrist, and Pulitzer prize-winning author from Harvard, emphasizes the point that there is a developing moral sense within a child.

I happen to think it is God-given, that there is a craving for a moral order. I would say the child has a need for "moral articulation" of what the world is all about, what it means, and what this life is about. This desire to figure out the world, to make sense of it, and in some way find meaning in life is built into each of us ... These questions are connected to one's nature as a human being.[9]

Clearly, it is best to guide the process of moral development in our children at an early age. But the growing involvement of adolescents in the more complex and sometimes dangerous aspects of our society increases their need to be able to make ethical decisions. Adolescence provides us with a major opportunity to listen and talk with them about moral and spiritual matters.

When talking to your teenager about moral and spiritual concerns:

• *Start by clarifying your own moral code and religious beliefs.* We can't give away what we don't have.

• *Avoid a condescending attitude or judgmental tone of voice.* When teenagers seem to reject their parents' religious views, the problem may not be the moral code or beliefs but how they are communicated. When youth specialist Jay Kesler spoke to a convention of twelve thousand young people, he wondered whether he could say anything about sexual morality that would be accepted by these teens. His speech was well received. One seventeen-year-old girl summed up the reason why.

"I was trying to figure out why I am not offended when you say some of the same things my folks say. I think it's that you don't talk down to us or at us. You always say 'we' rather than 'you' when talking about our problems."[10]

• *Do what you say.* Teens are quick to spot hypocrisy. This doesn't mean that we have to pretend to be perfect parents. No one is. But it does mean that we strive to act according to our values.

• *Admit your mistakes.* There is nothing worse or more foolish than a parent who presumes to be perfect or appear self-righteous. Our teens know us too well. On the other hand, there is nothing more persuasive about the rightness of our standards than when we admit we have failed to live up to our standards and say, "I'm sorry. I was wrong."

• *Talk about what you believe.* Most teenagers want to know what their parents believe, but many teenagers have told me that they don't really know what their parents think about God or the meaning of life. Yet, perhaps more than at any other time, these beliefs become important to the teen as reference points in their own decision making and behavior.

• *Don't force-feed your teen religion.* In an article on the problem of runaways, Dr. Norman Vincent Peale wrote, "The knowledge and love of God are life's greatest joy and privilege, but they can't be forced or hammered into anyone."[11]

Teenagers are attracted to what works. If they see that our faith gives us confidence to face problems, that forgiveness really is experienced and practiced, that our relationship to God fills our lives with joy and meaning, then sooner or later they will want the same.

The "Well-Rounded" Adolescent

While it's important to be aware of our teen's growth along these five dimensions of adolescent development, it is also very helpful to have a clear idea of what a healthy, happy, "well-rounded" adolescent might look like.

We can represent each of the five developmental areas as a spoke in a wheel. It's clear that when one or more areas are not developed, the wheel cannot turn smoothly. Healthy progress requires well-rounded development—and teens require attention and encouragement in all of these five areas.

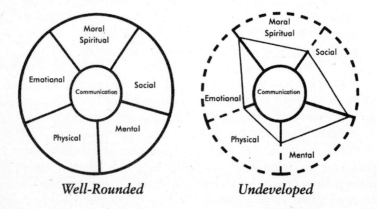

Well-Rounded   *Undeveloped*

Keep in mind that it is normal for the wheel to be out of round at different stages of the teen's development. No one develops at the same rate or in the same way along every dimension, and it is important not to rush the developmental process.

Caring communication (committed, empathetic, firm) is the hub supporting the spokes of well-rounded development. It is always at the center of a healthy, growing relationship.

Action Steps for Helping Your Teen Sail through Adolescence

• *Try to remember what it was like for you as a teenager.* What aspect of your physical development did you find most embarrassing as a teen? How did you feel about it? Do you think your parents knew what was bothering you? Did they ever discuss it with you? Think about what kind of involvement you would have liked your parents to have had, and compare it to how you've dealt with these issues with your teen. Your answers to these questions should give you a better idea of the uncertainties and embarrassments your child feels—and prepare you to offer the support and reassurance he or she needs.

• *In which of the five developmental areas do you think your teen needs the most support?* List five positive things that you can say that will support or reassure your teen in this area. Make sure to point out his or her successes or achievements in ways that will be acceptable and appreciated. For example, bragging about teens in front of their peers might be embarrassing, but the same story told to their grandparents might be just right.

• *On the circle that follows, plot where you think your teen is in each of the five areas by putting a dot on the line between 0 and 5.* Then connect the dots. This exercise will reveal areas that need further development and special encouragement.

• *On a new circle, plot where you think your teen was six months ago, to show the progress he or she has made, and where you'd like him or her to be six months from now, to help you set some goals for the future.* It may also be interesting to plot a profile of your own development when you were your teen's age. For example, do you see any similarities or differences in the social area? If you were outgoing and your daughter is shy, what can you share with her that will convey understanding and give her emotional strength? You might also want to ask your teen to plot where she thinks she fits on this wheel.

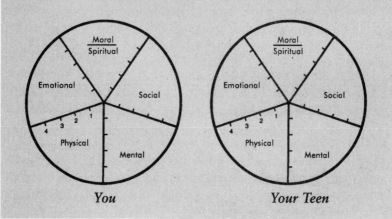

You

Your Teen

CHAPTER THREE

THE ELEMENTS OF EFFECTIVE COMMUNICATION

I know you believe you understand what you think I said,
but I'm not sure you realize
that what you heard is not what I meant.

— ANONYMOUS

We start talking to each other, but we finish screaming at each
other. Then I don't talk to them for about a week.

— JOHN, AGE 15

Most of us know as much about how communication works as we know about the mechanical principles that make the engines in our cars run—which is to say that we don't know very much. We get in our cars, turn on the engine, and drive away. We don't worry about how the motor works ... until it breaks down and leaves us stranded.

Most parents feel the same way about communication with their teens. They're perfectly willing just to start it up and hope it keeps on running smoothly. Perhaps because most of us think that communication is a natural human process that should run easily without much tinkering on our part, we tend to get discouraged when we run into difficulties. We feel as if our smoothly running communications "engine" has broken down without an owner's manual or a service station in sight. Only then do we feel the need to learn anything about how and why it works.

Although it's normal for communication to break down between parents and adolescents, these failures leave parents feeling terribly bewildered. Why would some teens escalate seemingly innocent remarks into huge problems? Why do parents' deliberate attempts at understanding their teens' problems sometimes backfire?

Just as a manual shows you how your office equipment works, with instructions on what to do when things go wrong, this chapter offers you an "owner's manual" to the communications process. It will answer questions about why communication sometimes breaks down, and help you analyze and avoid the more serious problems, offering tips for getting the process up and running again.

Although if will take some effort on your part, the communication process is not really difficult to understand. As I've noted elsewhere, sometimes it only takes slight adjustments—a little bit of lubrication here, a bit of fine tuning there—to solve the problems. With the right tools, clear directions, and a little time to practice, you can make the repairs you need.

What Is Communication?

Communication is … a laugh, a handshake, a tear, a frown, a gesture, a word, a kiss, a tone, a smile, a whisper, a scream, a wink, a pause, a grunt, a hug.

"Communication" comes from a Latin word meaning "to make common, to share." It refers to the process of transferring a message or meaning from one person's mind to the mind of another through your words, body language, and tone of voice. Actually, real communication doesn't take place until the person who hears your message interprets it correctly. Only then has there been a common meaning, a shared message, a meeting of the minds.

On the surface, this process can seem simple, a matter of pure habit. If you look "under the hood," though, you'll see that communication involves several "parts" all running together properly to make the whole process work. When you have a good conversation with someone, all these parts are in "motion" and interacting with and affecting each other, like the parts of a smoothly running engine. The whole process can get pretty complex. Let's simplify it by looking at each of the seven parts of the communication process.

The Seven Elements
of the Communication Process

As noted, the communication process can be broken down into seven distinct but interdependent elements.

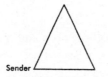

First, think of yourself as the *sender* of the message. As sender, you play the most important role in the process of communicating with your teen. Centuries ago, Aristotle stated that the *ethos* or personality of the sender was the most vital element in the successful transmission of a message. Nothing in today's research has contradicted this belief.

You need to understand that your success at getting through to your teen depends primarily on you. You'll have to take responsibility for initiating discussions and for changing the way you communicate—by developing your own patience, openness, and empathy.

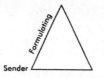

The next step in the communication process involves *formulating* a message from the ideas we want to communicate. You combine certain words, a tone of voice, a facial expression, posture, and so on, from the many options open to you into a unique message. This step in the process takes place very rapidly and almost automatically. We don't give it much thought—which often leads to communication problems. Often, the best way to improve communication is to spend more time thinking about how to formulate your message.

The result of this process is the *message*. This message is your expression of your ideas—the words and appearances you "transmit" to your teen. It's what he sees, feels, and hears as you speak.

Next, the person who has received our message *interprets* it. Unfortunately, his interpretation may not even be close to what you intended.

The *receiver* is the person who tries to understand the message you've sent—in this case, your teen. As the receiver, your teen's disposition, attitudes, and habits all influence the way he will interpret your messages.

Your teen's personality isn't the only determinant of how effective your message will be. The quality of your *relationship* with your teen also affects the process. Although a part of that relationship, perhaps a large part, is constant and cannot be easily changed, a small but significant part will change in each encounter, as you and your teen experience emotional ups and downs, successes and failures—adding a fresh, but unpredictable dynamic to the communication process.

The *context* in which our communications occur adds a further element of complexity to the process. Context includes the time, place, and circumstances in which your communication takes place—elements such as the presence of friends or the pressure of a final exam. The context directly affects what is said, how it is said, and how it is heard.

When you combine these seven parts, you can see how the process of transferring meaning fits together: The *sender formulates* an idea into a transmitted *message* that is *interpreted* by the *receiver* in reference to his *relationship* to the sender within a particular *context*.

A Seven-Step Repair Manual

How often have you wished that you had said something differently or not at all? Perhaps you've had to explain: "I didn't mean that the way it sounded" or "That wasn't what I meant at all." Such misunderstandings are common in most homes.

As the Chinese proverb reminds us, "Nobody's family can hang out the sign, 'Nothing the matter here.'" Every family has its communication problems. Given the varieties of interests, experiences, and inclinations that make up a family, it would be surprising to find a family that didn't have its share of disagreements and disputes.

You've just seen how the communication process can be broken down into seven key steps. Now we'll take a look at what you can do when something goes wrong with the communication process in your family—how you can respond to the typical problems that crop up in each of the seven steps.

As a ninth grader wrote in one of our surveys, "Some parents don't talk to their children because they're so afraid that if they say something wrong then everything will fall apart." By learning to recognize some of the common pitfalls, as well as how to respond to them, you can learn to be a more confident, more committed communicator. And commitment is necessary if you're going to discover and remedy the problems you face. Let's try to figure out what might be going wrong.

Problems with the Sender

Both speaker and listener play key roles in the success or failure of any communication. As the parent of a teenager, however, you often have to take the initiative for any discussions. This means that your role probably has the biggest influence on the outcome. Therefore, if you see that you're having trouble talking to your teen, the first place to look for problems is in your own behavior.

Most parents are too busy dealing with their day-to-day problems or taking care of their responsibilities at work or at home to really reflect on their relationship with their teen. They can find it extremely difficult to imagine how their actions look from the outside.

In my counseling work, I have found that many parents need help in understanding how the way they act affects their communication. One approach that seems to work is to analyze communication problems using a psychological method known as *transactional analysis*. Transactional analysis was developed by Eric Berne and later popularized in Thomas A. Harris' best-selling book, *I'm O.K., You're O.K.* According to this model, most people express themselves in one of three characteristic ways, which can be labeled as Parent, Adult, or Child. These labels describe the quality of the expression and are independent of the speaker's chronological age.

For the sake of this discussion, Parent expressions can be thought of as attempts to raise the status of the sender and belittle the status of the listener. This kind of expression includes scolding, condemning, yelling, lecturing, commanding, ordering, warning, criticizing, advising, put-downs, inattentiveness, anger, insensitivity, and a harsh tone of voice.

Adult expressions can be characterized as honest and nondefensive. They draw out the best in listeners and treat them as persons of equal worth. Adult expressions convey mutuality, respect, openness, sensitivity, directness, a readiness to listen, and an honest expression of feelings.

Child expressions are sometimes spontaneous, lively, and fun-loving—except when the individual doesn't get his own way. All of us act childish at times. In the Child mode we want to be served and coddled, to be the center of attention, free of responsibility. Child expressions are characterized by emotional outbursts, anger, frustration, irresponsibility, talking too much, dogmatic attitudes, unclear meanings, vengeful desires, and unfair comparisons.

Naturally, the way someone expresses herself (as Parent, Adult, or Child) will influence the way her listener responds. Most conversations follow one of the three patterns shown in the diagram that follows:

Sender		Listener
Parent		Parent
Adult		Adult
Child		Child

In almost every case, Adult to Adult expressions are a better basis for productive communications. Adult expressions encourage the listener to reciprocate with Adult expressions—reinforcing good communication practices in both the speaker and the listener. Parent and Child modes of expression, on the other hand, tend to block communication. Parent expressions influence the listener to respond with Child expressions, and Child expressions influence the listener to respond in a Parent mode. In both cases, the paired styles of expression (Parent-Child) reinforce conversational styles that can destroy or disrupt the communication process.

Like most psychological theories, transactional analysis offers a simple way of understanding a complicated problem. However, given the unique background of the relationship between parent and teen, stretching from infancy to near-adulthood, it's not surprising that this approach can be so helpful.

If you're not aware that you are taking part in Adult/Parent/Child transactions, you can become bitterly entangled in a network of unpleasant arguments and bad feelings without the foggiest notion of how to get out. On the other hand, if you can use this method to understand how your style affects your teen's responses—you can begin to change your Parent-style messages into Adult-style messages, which will, in turn, reinforce Adult responses from your teen.

Repair Strategies for the Sender

How can you tell whether the problem is with the sender? If you're like most parents, you're getting plenty of feedback from your teen on just how good a job you're doing. If your teen complains that you're "treating him like a baby" or that "all you do is yell," you should look more closely into your contribution to the problem. You can always ask your teen (if you're brave) or a trusted relative or family friend for feedback on your performance as a "sender."

• *Analyze yourself.* In conversations that don't seem to work, ask yourself: "Am I expressing myself like a Parent, a Child, or an Adult? How do I want to come across? How do I need to change my message to get the effect I want?"

• *Act in the present.* Keep in mind that there's a connection between your past experiences and the style (Parent, Adult, or Child) that you choose today. It may be difficult to give up the patterns you've grown up with, but it is possible. Recognizing the communication style you now use, and making a conscious decision to move beyond it to use an Adult style, can be an important step toward improving communication with your teen.

• *Be sensitive to your Parent behavior—and work on adopting an Adult replacement.* Avoid using Parent words like "should," "always," "never," "stupid," or "grow up" or a Child vocabulary punctuated by "I want …," "I need …," "I wish …," "I won't …," "I can't …," etc. Instead, use Adult expressions that convey openness, flexibility, assertiveness, and sensitivity to your teen's point of view. For example, "What do you think?" "We might …," "Let's try to …," "It seems best to …," "What if …," etc.

• *Draw out your teen's best qualities.* You can encourage your teen to shift from a Child or Parent mode to an Adult mode by maintaining your own Adult style even when he or she acts obnoxiously. Don't repay destructive talk with destructive talk. Keep in mind that what you "send" in conversation can change and improve what you "receive."

Problems with the Formulating Process

One of the most common causes of parent/teen miscommunication is that our messages aren't clear. This happens because although we know what we mean to say, we don't always know how to express our meaning in a way that others can easily understand.

There are four basic reasons why we fail to formulate clear messages.

First, we assume that our words can have only one meaning— the one we intend. In fact, it's often possible to interpret a given string of words any number of ways. For example, the five hundred most common words in the English language have a combined total of over fourteen thousand different meanings—an average of more than twenty-eight meanings per word.

Second, your teen brings his or her individual experience and point of view to the task of interpreting your words. For example, you may intend the simple message "I want you home at a reasonable hour" to mean that your teenager should be home before 11:00 P.M. Your teen may interpret "reasonable" to mean 1:00 A.M.

Third, when we make a statement, we may not include every detail that we have in mind, because we assume that some of the connections are self-evident. Our teens, however, may miss the implications altogether. For example:

What I Said	**What I Meant**
Jud, please mow the grass.	Jud, please mow the grass this morning because it looks as if it is going to rain this afternoon.

Unless I make clear exactly what I mean, Jud is left to fill in the thought on his own. Like any normal teenager, he is more likely to complete my thought as: "Jud, please mow the grass *sometime*."

Fourth, sometimes we are *deliberately* unclear because we are trying to be *indirect*. Indirect communication can be fun. Parents and teens both enjoy communicating through hints, facial expressions, inside references, and long-running jokes. It's fun to feel like an insider, but sometimes families overdo it—running the risk that some family members will be left in a fog. A good rule of thumb is that if an issue is complicated, or very important to one family member, or likely to hurt someone's feelings, the indirect expressions should be put aside.

Parents sometimes have an incentive to be indirect as they formulate their expressions. Indirectness gives them a way out of a difficult situation. If a statement backfires, the parent can always claim, "I didn't mean that!"

In general, indirectness promotes misunderstandings and develops a communication pattern that is dishonest, weak, and counterproductive.

Repair Strategies for the Formulating Process

If you and your teen consistently have trouble understanding one another, there's at least an even chance that some of your problem is coming from the formulation process.

• Analyze your statements to see whether the problem is in the way you formulate them. Ask yourself:

"Have I used any words or phrases that could possibly be misunderstood or interpreted in different ways?"

"Is my statement vague enough that my teen could interpret it differently than I intended it?"

"Have I left out details that might help my teen understand what I meant?"

"Have I used inside references or jargon that might be confusing to my teen?"

• If you're concerned that you're not formulating your statements to your teen clearly, think about these questions before you speak:

"What do I really want to say?"

"If someone made this statement to me, how would I interpret it?"

"What words and facial expressions will best convey that meaning?"

"Am I making any unwarranted assumptions?"

"Am I being clear and direct?"

Problems with the Message

How can you create messages that your teen will listen to and understand? The key is to pay as much attention to how you say the message—your tone of voice and facial expressions—as to the words that you say. How much of your message gets across is very closely tied to the way you present it.

Albert Mehrabian, a communications researcher at UCLA, startled people with the results of his extensive research, which showed that a spoken message affects the listener in the following ways:

• What you say—your word message—accounts for only 7 percent of what is believed.

- The way you say it—your tone of voice—accounts for 38 percent.
- The way you act while speaking—the nonverbal messages you send—accounts for an incredible 55 percent of what your listener will believe.[1]

The following diagram depicts the comparative impact of the verbal, tonal, and visual aspects of the messages you send.

Message Impact

Each of these three aspects of your message can have either a positive or a negative effect on your communication. The following list shows typical examples of different aspects of messages and indicates whether they'll tend to be received positively or negatively.

If you want to improve your communication with your teen, it's vital that you know how your messages are being received. Check the examples that follow that you honestly think are closest to the way you actually communicate with your teen. Then, when you feel brave enough, ask your teen to check the items he thinks are typical of your communication style. This exercise can be a real eye-opener—and can give you valuable feedback on how well your attempts to communicate are working. Remember, what your teen thinks you said is more important than what you meant to say.

Word Messages

Positive Word Messages
___I like the way you …
___Tell me about it.
___I'd like to hear more.
___How can I help?
___You must have felt really frustrated.
___I love you.

Negative Word Messages
___Don't be ridiculous!
___How many times must I tell you?
___You never …
___Are you crazy?
___That's stupid!
___You always …

Tone of Voice Messages

Positive Tone Messages Sound
___caring	___concerned	___joyful
___affirming	___cheerful	___relaxed
___supportive	___tender	___calm
___loving	___objective	___satisfied

Negative Tone Messages Sound
___sarcastic	___blaming	___emotional
___harsh	___rejecting	___scared
___judgmental	___hard	___tense
___angry	___frustrated	___blaring

Nonverbal Messages

Positive Signals
___smile	___eye contact	___touching
___head nod	___open arms	___relaxed body
___attentive face	___forward lean	___moving closer

Negative Signals
___rude gesture	___frown	___smirk
___crying	___jabbing	___disgust
___pointing	___hands thrown up	___moving away

Repair Strategies for the Message

Problems with the message can be fairly easy to identify. If you hear statements like, "That's not what you said," "It's not what you said, it's the tone of voice you used," or "You act like you couldn't be less interested in what I have to say," from your teen, getting better control over your words, your tone of voice, and the nonverbal aspects of your messages should be one of your top priorities. Consider the following strategies for improvement:

• *Words*: Pause before you start talking. Taking an extra second or two to consider the words you want to use—or not use—will help you avoid "conversation killers" and pick the words that make your point most accurately and effectively.

• *Tone of voice*: Try to hear your own tone of voice the way it sounds to your teen. It couldn't hurt to tape record a few of your conversations with your teen to get a really accurate picture. (Ask your teen first to make sure he doesn't mind. If you explain why you're taping, he's almost sure to go along.) Ask yourself whether your tone of voice conveys or reinforces the message you intended to send. Did it produce the effect you wanted?

• *Nonverbal signals*: Again, try to be aware of your body and facial expressions to see them in the same way your teen does. Videotape a conversation, or watch yourself in a mirror if possible. Ask yourself, "Do I look relaxed, confident, accepting, open to my teen's feelings?" If you don't look relaxed or open, simply try to talk yourself into the right frame of mind by repeating, "Relax!" or "Be open!" It's amazing how this kind of self-talk can change the way you deliver your messages.

Problems with the Interpretation Process

If your teen can't interpret your messages properly, it's very unlikely that your intentions will get through. The process of interpretation is really your teen's responsibility, but there are things you can do to help your teen learn to interpret your communications more accurately.

The first step is to help her better understand your own communication style. One way to do this is to point out the communication-related strengths, weaknesses, idiosyncrasies, and special sensitivities that you've discovered as you've read through this book. (She might also learn a lot by reading it on her own.) If you think an argument or disagreement is linked to a misinterpretation, take the initiative for clarifying the problem before you proceed. Check to see whether she is, in fact, interpreting your statements correctly, clear up any immediate misunderstandings, and take advantage of the opportunity to reinforce the Adult-to-Adult nature of your communication styles.

The second step is to teach your teen to ask you to clarify points she doesn't understand. Teenagers tend to take expressions of lack of interest or ambivalence much more seriously than adults do—as if they were personal attacks. In many cases, they aren't sure how to find out whether they've misunderstood you. They're as afraid as you are of making things worse by asking. Let them know that you are willing to explain anything you've said or to clear up any impression they've received from your tone of voice or your nonverbal gestures, posture, or other behavior.

Keep in mind that when your teen fails to interpret what you said in the way you intended, she did not intend to misunderstand you. Don't make her feel guilty for misunderstanding. Let her know that if she's really interested in better communication, she must check with you about messages she isn't sure about or feels are unnecessarily negative, insulting, or hurtful.

Some teens discover that understanding your messages clearly and unambiguously isn't always in their interest. In most cases, though, your teen will discover that learning to interpret messages more clearly and accurately can be truly rewarding—both as an indication of her maturity and as a communication skill she can apply in all aspects of her life.

Repair Strategies for the Interpretation Process

As with the formulation process, problems with the interpretation process can be identified when you or your teen systematically misunderstand what the other is saying. It may not really matter whether the problem is one of formulation or interpretation. The two processes are closely related, and flaws in one can be overcome by working harder on the other.

• *Be alert to responses that suggest your teen is not interpreting you correctly.* If something about his reaction doesn't feel right, ask, "Do you know what I mean?" or say, "I'm not sure I'm being clear on this point. Let me try again to say what I mean."

• *Analyze a message that caused an emotional outburst in your teen.* What do you think caused the outburst? Do you think he interpreted your message correctly? What could you have done to make sure that he received the message you wanted to send? Think about ways to change your message to fit your teen's interpretation style, as well as ways to help him learn to interpret your messages better.

• *Analyze current disputes with your teen.* Does he seem to share interpretation problems? If so, try to involve your teen in a discussion of how failures in the communication process are getting in the way of the two of you really addressing the issues you care about. Keep in mind that as the sender of these parent/teen messages, you have a greater responsibility for how the message is received than does the interpreter. After all, the sender has almost complete flexibility in the form and timing of the message, as well as time to reflect on the best way to send it. The receiver, on the other hand, is put on the spot—with only a relatively limited number of possible responses. The real danger of interpretation problems is that they can lead to incorrect assumptions—such as, "my son is lazy" or "my dad is unreasonable"—that can lead to a vicious, self-fulfilling circle of misunderstandings.

Problems with the Receiver

Many parents feel that their teens change more often than the weather. One mother told me that her daughter can be ranting and raving one minute and calm and sweet the next. Teenagers are in the middle of one of the most dynamic and turbulent periods of their life. As they grow and change, how they feel from one day to the next—if not from one moment to the next—has a powerful influence on how they receive our messages.

Teens often don't understand what they feel—or the stages they're going through—well enough to control their emotions or their expressions. They say things they don't mean. They mean things they don't say. They are so preoccupied with figuring themselves out that they don't listen very well. They can scream hatred at their parents and yet at the same time be fiercely loyal to them. They can think so highly of themselves or so little of themselves that our opinions may not matter. Unfortunately, teens change so fast, and need so much patience and understanding, that parents can easily get discouraged.

Keep in mind that things are never as bad as they seem. After all, your parents probably felt some of the same frustrations, and you didn't turn out all that badly. And there are still several things we can do that will help our teens to understand us.

Repair Strategies to Help the Receiver

Problems with the receiver are the most difficult to identify and remedy. After all, it's rare that just one person is to blame for problems in parent/teen communication, and your teen is just learning how to interpret the increasingly complicated messages he's receiving from you and others in his near-adult world.

• *Relax.* You can't really control how your teen receives your messages. Keep in mind that your teen is something of a moving target, growing and changing constantly. Even if you did figure out a foolproof way to reach him today, if might not work tomorrow. But keep in mind too that your teen is in the process of developing the patterns he'll live by as an adult. Do what you can to shape the receiver he will be in the future by reinforcing good communication practices whenever possible. Remember, time is on your side.

• *Remember.* Think back to your own experiences as an adolescent, and how your preoccupations sometimes screened out what your parents said. Which "distractions" interfered with your communication with your parents the most? Do you see these patterns or distractions in your own teen's behavior? When you were a teenager, how did you want your parents to respond to your failure to hear their messages? The best response is probably just to be patient. If your message is really important, try repeating it in another way, on another day.

• *Reflect.* Put yourself in your teen's shoes for a moment. How would you receive the messages you've sent as a parent? What would make you pay attention to the messages? What would help you interpret them correctly?

Problems with the Relationship

When my son Jud's choir returned home from an eleven-day concert tour through Tennessee, Virginia, and Washington, DC, they put on a final performance for parents and friends. I thought the concert was superb, exciting, moving! The following week my family and I attended another choir concert—this one given by another group of teenagers on tour. To me, the second concert seemed unduly long and boring. What was the real difference between the two concerts? The most likely answer is that my relationship with Jud determined my response.

The quality of your relationship with your teen has a powerful influence over how well you communicate. When your relationship is good, you'll be more open, more receptive, and affirming. When it isn't, you'll be more critical and less tolerant. Your teen's attitude can also play a role: Even if you feel very good about your relationship, your teenager may nurse a grudge or resentment. Paradoxically, the stronger your relationship is, the more willing you'll be to work on its problems. But if the relationship is weak, you'll be tempted to give up trying to make it better.

It makes sense, then, doesn't it, that building a strong relationship can be a key factor in developing better communication with your teen.

Repair Strategies for the Relationship

Almost every communication problem can be solved or at least moderated by building a stronger relationship. Relationship-building methods are discussed throughout this book. Every family is different, and you'll have to identify which of these are most likely to work for you. Try a few to see whether they make a difference, and keep trying until you see a definite improvement in your relationship with your teen.

• *Building mutual understanding and respect is one of the most powerful ways to build a stronger relationship.* One of the best ways to put this principle into practice is to make sure that you use "I" statements rather than "you" statements when you talk to your teen.

Using "I" statements offers a way to express your feelings without blaming or accusing your teen. It shows your respect for your teen and your willingness to hear their side of the story. As a result, your teen will be less defensive and be more likely to understand the point you're trying to get across. Imagine how different the effect of each of the following statements would be on your teen.

"You" Statements	"I" Statements
"You make me frustrated."	"I feel very frustrated."
"You haven't done what I asked you to do."	"I get upset when things I asked you to do are left undone."
"You make me so mad that I don't want to talk to you!"	"I feel too angry right now to talk constructively. Let's continue our conversation later."

• *If you get into an argument or disagreement with your teen, be careful not to let the dispute hurt the relationship.* Let your teen know that despite your feelings at that moment, you want your relationship to be a strong, positive one over time.

For example, you might say:

"I think that we are having a difficult time accepting each other right now. But I want you to know that even though your behavior really bothers me, deep down I accept you. I want us to resolve this problem. Let's take a break and talk again in an hour."

Problems with the Context

I recently overheard an argument between a father and his teen-ager. The boy had just come home from mowing a lawn. He was hot, sweaty, and exhausted. The father was exasperated that his son hadn't done something he'd been asked to do. Neither was ready to listen to the other or even be civil. The result was predictable—a nasty exchange of angry words that could not help but damage their relationship. Perhaps if they had waited until they were both ready to discuss the issues calmly, this relationship could have been saved.

This is a good example of how important context is to the success or failure of communication. Words or statements that are effective in one situation can have terrible results in another. Choosing the right environment or right time for a discussion can make a world of difference.

Trying to understand, evaluate, predict or create the proper context for a given conversation can be a difficult exercise, because you don't control a number of the variables that can affect communication, and you may not be able to wait for the perfect moment. You should always, however, keep in mind the influence that the context has on how successful your communication will be.

The context for a given situation includes a broad range of influences—how comfortable the physical setting is, what distractions can get in the way, how strong the parent/teen relationship is, how well recent disagreements have been handled, what other deadlines or concerns you or your teen are facing, and so on.

There are two basic directions you can take if you face context problems. You might want to delay or reschedule an important discussion if you or your teen are tired, busy with a project, studying or reading the paper, trying to solve some other problem, watching TV, in the presence of friends or other people, not feeling well physically, or depressed or moody. You could also try scheduling discussions ahead of time so that you can influence or improve the environment or the state of mind of the participants.

Repair Strategies for the Context

Problems with context are easy to spot. If you feel distracted, tired, unwilling to exert yourself, or preoccupied with other concerns it's unlikely that you'll be an effective communicator.

• *Keep your eyes open for the warning signs mentioned above.* When these conditions exist, you might delay the discussion by saying: "I need to discuss something with you, but I can see this is not a good time. When can we talk?"

• *If your teen is too tired, too upset, or too distracted to talk, give her the empathy she needs.* For example, "I sense you are very tired. Right?" Let her know that you respect and acknowledge her feelings. Ask yourself: "If I were in my teen's situation, how would I want my parents to respond to me?" It may not be the right time to talk, but it could be the perfect time to strengthen your relationship.

• *Your context for any given conversation will be different from your teen's.* You'll have had different experiences, different moods, and different physical conditions during the time before you came together to talk. Before you start the conversation, you need to consider not only whether the time and place are right for you, but also whether they're right for your teen. You can always ask whether it's a good time for her.

If you decide to proceed, it can only help you to know how your teen is feeling, and what her day's been like. You might also want to let her know a little bit about your context. She may get valuable insight into what you're saying and how your context affects the way you say it.

Reaching Your Destination

Communication is one of the most complicated and most sophisticated of human activities. Communication at its best takes place as part of a calm, uninterrupted, casual discussion. Unfortunately, parents and teens tend to bring all kinds of busy schedules, strong emotions, and mixed agendas to their communication process. Teens want to convince their parents of their maturity and need for independence, while parents want to protect their children and make sure that their teens know how they're expected to act. Given these conflicting interests, is it any wonder that parents and teens sometimes don't communicate as well as they could?

You cannot force your teen to respond exactly the way you want, but you can take responsibility for your communications in a way that makes a difference—by increasing your understanding of how communication works, developing a working knowledge of the seven-step "repair manual," and letting your teen know that you will go the extra mile to reach a mutually satisfying destination.

You might not reach your destination immediately. The son of a friend of mine couldn't stand his father's brand of discipline. As soon as he was old enough, he "escaped" it by joining the Marines! Six months later the son called his father and said,

"Dad, there are several men in my group who can't take the pressure. They're falling like flies. The only reason I'm still here is that you taught me the value of discipline. Thanks for hanging in there, Dad."

Repairing your communication breakdowns may be too difficult for you to do alone. If you try the methods in this chapter without success, you should seek out the help of a certified clinical psychologist or a pastor, priest, or rabbi trained in family counseling. The additional reading on parent-teen communication listed at the back of this book can also be helpful. Do whatever it takes to make communication work for you and your teen.

Action Steps for Repairing Communication Breakdowns

- *If you want to become more skilled at understanding your communications problems, analyze your last few disputes with your teens according to the seven-element model.* Look for each of the elements in your personal experience, and try to identify which of the "parts broke down" in each case.

- *It's rare that a breakdown of only one of the seven elements disrupts communications.* Given the complexity of the process and the interrelationships and interdependencies of the parts, it's much more likely that a few or most of the elements are involved. Map out which elements are typically involved in your communications problems, looking for patterns that you and your teen can use to develop strategies for fixing the process.

- *Looking at the transactional analysis diagram shown earlier in the chapter, decide which of the three possible patterns best represents the transactions you have with your teen.* Show the diagram to your teen and ask for her opinion of your choice. If your pattern includes either Parent or Child roles, review the strategies for repair in that section and take steps to correct the problem.

- *Ask your teen about how your messages are received in terms of your choice of words, nonverbal signals, and tone of voice.* Show him the chart of message characteristics that appeared earlier in the chapter, if he needs suggestions. Ask your spouse or a friend who will be honest with you to help you make the adjustments you need to make.

- *If your communication with your teen is often affected by contextual problems—problems related to bad timing, a noisy or busy environment, distractions, or interruptions—work with your teen to set up a context that encourages free, honest, and open expression.* This can range from scheduling a walk together or agreeing to move to another room of the house for discussions to going out for something to eat or even taking a trip together.

CHAPTER FOUR

FIVE KEYS TO COMMUNICATING WITH YOUR TEENAGER

Dad, it would be helpful to me if you would look at me instead of the paper when we are talking. We could finish our conversation quicker.

— JUD SWETS AT AGE 13

Why is it so hard to get through to teenagers? Could it be for some of the same reasons teens have a hard time getting through to us? One of the most common complaints from teenagers is that even though they want to communicate with their parents, they are turned off by what their parents say and how they say it. Or, as in my case, by the way they don't listen.

Do you really need to earn the right to be heard by your teenager? Isn't this right guaranteed simply by the fact that you're the parent? And haven't you already earned that right by the thousands of hours and dollars you've spent on her throughout her childhood—caring for him or her during sickness, providing her clothes, room, and board, driving her millions of miles to practices, piano lessons, and ballet? Yes! In theory ...

In real life, things don't always work according to the theory. Adolescents are firmly rooted in the present. While they can keep track of millions of details about what's happened to them during the past week, they can't be expected to remember all the sacrifices you've made for them over the past decade and a half or so. They can't recall your pain at their birth. They don't see the mountains of love and energy that have gone into ensuring their healthy development.

In the real world—despite the unfairness of the situation— parents need to earn the right to be heard if they want to maintain open, healthy communication with their teenager. And, in spite of all the difficulties, sometimes you'll manage to make it work. Maybe you'll say the right thing at the right time. Maybe you'll say the right thing in words that your teen finds easy to accept, rather than in the way you first formulated it. Maybe you'll get tired of waiting for your teen to grow more thoughtful, more even-tempered, and more mature—and take the initiative for creating better communication yourself.

How can you increase the frequency of these communication breakthroughs? We got a good start by learning the basics of communication and how it works. Next we'll look at five key strategies that can make your communication links stronger. These five strategies are general rules that can be applied every day and in almost every situation. If you already have a strong relationship with your teenager, you'll find examples of these five strategies in your everyday behavior. If you're looking to strengthen or build your relationship, these five rules make an excellent blueprint! They'll help you sail past the barriers to conversation. They'll help you develop feelings of closeness with your teen and put you in a position to help him thrive despite the turbulence of his adolescent years.

Show Genuine Interest in Your Teen's Situation

In an interview with journalist Ann McCarroll, fifteen-year-old Bob said that he had "some mother!" He explained:

"Each morning she sits with me while I eat breakfast. We talk about anything and everything. She isn't refined or elegant or educated. She's a terrible housekeeper. She uses double negatives. But she's interested in everything I do and she listens to me—even if she's busy or tired."[1]

Spending time, showing interest, listening, talking about "anything and everything"—this is the kind of behavior that can earn you the right to be heard. It's as simple as adapting your time and conversation to the interests and attitudes of our teenagers, as Bob's mother did. It's really not all that hard to tune into your teen's interests. Ask yourself the following questions:

"What activities/experiences is my teen involved in?"
"How does my teen really feel about these involvements?"
"How can I best draw out my teen's thoughts and feelings on these subjects?"
"What issues do we really need to talk about?"

This exercise can generate a surprising number of ideas to discuss with your teen and questions to ask that will show your genuine interest.

In addition, you need to learn to really listen to your teen's answers. Although we'll cover listening techniques more fully in a separate chapter, it is important to keep in mind that listening well is a key element in earning the right to be heard. Listening well takes tremendous discipline. You need to learn to focus on your teen, not on yourself. When your teen needs you to listen, it's crucial that you've committed yourself not to argue or counter every comment with your own ideas.

If you're lucky, all of this work on listening will be rewarded through the principle of "mutual exchange." As a child, you probably heard this expressed as, "If you hit me, I'll hit you back!" In communicating with your teen, the principle of mutual exchange should work this way: "If I genuinely listen, I will create an atmosphere in which my teen is likely to listen to me."

"But I never seem to get equal time," you may say. Again, there are no guarantees. Adolescents need to spend an inordinate amount of time keeping track of their thoughts, feelings, and schedules, not to mention what's happening in the lives of their peers. These things take an enormous amount of mental energy. You may have to wait until your teen's personal busyness is under better control before you receive the full measure of respect and responsiveness you deserve.

A common mistake parents make is to think that we can win our teens over simply with money or gifts. It doesn't work. The only gifts your teen really needs from you are your continuing love and attention. When you offer these gifts through your willingness to genuinely listen, then you'll win the right to be heard.

Develop a Clear Purpose

We all say things we wish we could retract. The human tongue often seems to function without purpose or direction, like a ship without a rudder, or a restless stallion without a bridle (James 3:2-6). The words fly out of our mouths before we consider their effect. We might get some temporary relief from lashing out. But at what cost? Terrible damage can be done when we speak without a thought-through purpose.

Purpose makes it possible for us to rein in our runaway tirades or pontifications. If we have a positive goal in mind, then we'll get our message across, despite the influence of stormy emotions or difficult situations. As writer Norman Cousins puts it, "Effective communications, oral or written, depend absolutely on a clear understanding of one's purpose. That purpose should be clearly identified."[2]

As I reflect on this statement, I realize that I have developed very clear communication goals that guide what I say to my son and daughter. I don't always follow them, but I know that I would "slip up" a lot more without the following goals:

1. To speak to my teens in such a way that their self-esteem is enhanced, so that they feel good about themselves and have confidence in their ability to solve problems.

2. To listen to my teens in such a way that they know that I care about them—care enough to make a serious effort to understand them.

3. To let my teens know that what they say and how they feel is important to me, even when I disagree.

4. To work at achieving mutual understanding through honest feedback.

5. To communicate my concerns about negative behavior with firmness, but without put-downs or recriminations.

6. To send a clear message to my teens that I love them, and that their well-being is as important to me as my own.

As part of the process of building better communication with your teens, you'll want to try to develop some general guidelines like these that you can apply in your own family. Clear-cut goals make it possible to sort out the conflicting emotions and necessities that accompany adolescence. With your goals in mind, you'll know when to intervene and when to let things pass; when to take the initiative and when to leave the initiative to your teen. Goals make it possible to evaluate your response or your options according to larger issues, instead of the convenience or the panic of the moment.

My ability to influence my teens through their period of adolescence is too important to me for me not to have clear destinations and self-directing goals constantly in mind.

Avoid Conversation Killers

Every parent has had the following experience: A conversation with their teen is going along perfectly smoothly when, suddenly, it comes to an abrupt conclusion. Teens are notoriously sensitive to what their parents say and how they say it, and they will "break the connection" if they feel slighted, patronized, or ordered around—a disconcerting but predictable reaction, when you come to understand it. Avoid "conversation killers." Conversation killers take one or more of the following forms: incessant talking, contradictions, put-downs, dogmatic statements, a judgmental tone of voice, unfair generalizations, and responses that reveal that you're not listening. For example:

"No, it cost $5.50, not $4.50."
"Hey dummy, what did I just tell you to do?"
"You idiot!"
"You are a terrible driver."
"When will you grow up?"

To learn how to avoid killing a conversation, check yourself on each of the following questions by circling Yes or No.

Yes No Do I talk longer than a minute without giving my teen a chance to speak? (Time yourself.)

Yes No Do I talk about my self or my interests more than I listen to my teen's interests?

Yes No Do I correct or contradict on nonessential matters when I think my teen's ideas are wrong?

Yes No Do I assume that getting the facts straight is more important than understanding feelings?

Yes No Do I call my teen names that, regardless of my intention, could be interpreted as uncomplimentary?

Yes No Do I tend to tease or "get back" at my teen by the things I say or the way I say them?

Yes No Do I tend to be dogmatic or argumentative?

Yes No Does my teen feel that I think that I am always right?

Yes No Does my teen think the tone of my voice sounds harsh or disapproving?

Yes No Do I find myself not knowing or understanding what my teen has just said?

It is not easy to see yourself clearly and admit your mistakes, but this kind of honest self-examination may help you see what your teen sees. Reflect on the questions you answered yes to. They all point to the use of conversation killers. Now think about how your teen reacts when you act this way in conversation. Most conversation killing is inadvertent and persists because the "killer" isn't even aware of the problem. Now that you have some idea of what the problem is, you should be able to learn to catch yourself *before* the damage is done. Think about other conversation killers that have interrupted your conversations with your teen. It may take some time before you're able to rid your conversation of these destructive elements—but you'll be rewarded with a much better conversational atmosphere.

Control Your Emotions

We all overreact at times. While it may be possible to pull something positive out of these occasional eruptions of feelings, most of us would probably agree that we need to learn how to control our emotions—especially how we express them—to maintain healthy communication with our teens.

Maintaining our self-control is especially difficult when our teens lose theirs—and take their frustrations out on us. We'll deal with this issue in more detail later in the book, but here are some basic strategies you can use to get started:

• *Call a "time out" when the emotions get too hot.* When you notice that tempers are starting to flare, you can say, "Let's take a break and talk more in an hour."

• *Accept responsibility for your behavior.* This is basic. Our tendency is to blame others when things go wrong. We may see this most clearly in our children when they try to pin the blame for what they have done on others. To give your teen a good example of taking responsibility for controlling your emotions, you could say, for example, "Remember when I said ...? I was wrong. I'm sorry." If you don't accept responsibility for your behavior, neither will your children.

• *Respond to your teen's frustrating behavior by taking a positive action before you lose your temper.* For example, "I am unhappy to see you watching TV when you have so much homework to do. I would like you to turn it off until your work is done." As the diagram that follows shows, the longer you wait, the harder you'll find it to respond objectively.

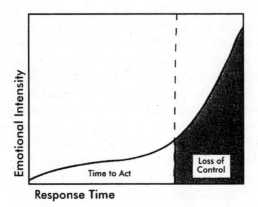

• *Keep in mind that you're at your best as a parent when you've had enough rest.* This may seem obvious, but fatigue causes or fuels more communication problems than you probably realize. You are simply not at your best when you're tired. If a problem comes up when you're exhausted, take a break for a quick nap to enhance your ability to listen and talk effectively. On this point my son comments, "It's better to rest for twenty minutes and talk for ten than to argue for thirty."

• *Use "I" messages instead of "you" messages.* "I" messages take some of the sting out of the message, and typically don't cause as much of a defensive reaction. For example:

"You" Messages	"I" Messages
"You never do what I ask you to do! You make me so angry! You never remember to take my tools inside!"	"I feel frustrated when you don't do what I ask you to do. I am angry, son. This is the third time my tools have been left outside."

"I" messages can help you release your feelings without condemning your teen or destroying your relationship.

If you find that you cannot control your emotions, you may need to seek professional help. You may be abusing your child verbally, if not physically. Getting help from a pastor or qualified counselor is not a sign of weakness—it is a sign of strength. The real weaklings are those who refuse to admit that they have a problem—or try to ignore it, cover it up, or blame others. Often just talking about the problem with someone who can listen skillfully will relieve some of the problem. Talking it out can help us gain a new perspective on our relationship with our teen and move forward.

Invest Time with Your Teen

According to one study, men spent twice as much time with their children in 1980 as they did in 1960. Unfortunately, that means that the time they spent had risen from six to twelve minutes per day. These fathers were taking only twelve minutes a day to establish understanding, to really listen, to transfer significant values!

Do we really need much time to communicate well? If we don't make the time, we can't listen. If we don't listen, we can't show teens the acceptance they need. If they don't feel accepted, they can't develop self-esteem. If they don't develop self-esteem, they can't learn to communicate in an open and caring way, and we can't earn the right to be heard.

Perhaps you know Sandy and Harry Chapin's song "Cat's in the Cradle." This song has had a strong impact on my life. For many years it has helped remind me of my need to invest "quality time" in my relationship with my children.

My child arrived just the other day;
he came to the world in the usual way.
But there were planes to catch and bills to pay;
he learned to walk while I was away.
And he was talkin' 'fore I knew it,
and as he grew he'd say,
"I'm gonna be like you, Dad,
you know I'm gonna be like you."

Chorus
And the cat's in the cradle and the silver spoon,
little boy blue and the man in the moon.
"When you comin' home, Dad?"
"I don't know when, but we'll get together then;
you know we'll have a good time then."

My son turned ten just the other day;
he said, "Thanks for the ball, Dad, come on
let's play. Can you teach me to throw?"
I said, "Not today, I got a lot to do."
He said, "That's okay." And he,
he walked away, but his smile
never dimmed, it said, "I'm gonna be
like him, yeah, you know I'm gonna be like him."

Chorus

Well he came from college just the other day;
so much like a man I just had to say,
"Son, I'm proud of you, can you sit for awhile?"
He shook his head and he said with a smile,
"What I'd really like, Dad, is to borrow the car keys;
see you later, can I have them please?"

Chorus

I've long since retired, my son's moved away;
I called him up just the other day.
I said, "I'd like to see you if you don't mind."
He said, "I'd love to, Dad, if I can find the time.
You see, my new job's a hassle and the kids
have the flu, but it's sure nice talkin' to you,
Dad, it's been sure nice talking to you."
And as I hung up the phone, it occurred to me,
he'd grown up just like me;
my boy was just like me.[3]

This is a powerful song with an important message. It made me stop and reconsider how my children fit into my priorities. Does it have the same effect on you?

How will you find the time in your busy schedule? The answer, of course, is that you won't "find" the time; you need to make it. Here are a few simple techniques that will help you focus on what matters most.

• *Control the TV before it controls you.* The A.C. Nielsen Company has reported that the average American television set is on for forty-three hours and fifty-two minutes per week. That's more than six hours a day. In her excellent book *Traits of a Healthy Family*, Dolores Curran writes:

> *Whether the breakdown in family communication leads people to excessive viewing or whether excessive television breaks into family lives so pervasively as to literally steal it from them, we don't know ... But we do know that we can become out of reach to one another when we're in front of a TV set.*[4]

• *Pay more attention to scheduling your time.* In today's fast-paced world, you'll find that large portions of your time are taken away—stolen forever—by activities that "demand" your time but that aren't valuable or significant to you. It might help to list a full week's worth of your activities on paper, including everything from time spent on the phone to time spent with your teen. Organize the items on your list according to their importance to you. You'll be shocked at how much of your time goes to events or activities that you feel little interest in. Try to "free" as much of this underutilized time as you can—and use it to schedule more time with your teenager—talking, shopping, going out to lunch, or just doing chores around the house. I find my teens are usually ready to talk at night. All I need to do is to help get a snack, pull up a chair, and talk and listen like a friend.

• *Make the most of mealtime conversation.* According to Dr. Lee Salk, Cornell University's popular child psychologist, many people neglect to do this. He writes, "People used to talk and listen at meal time, but now they sit in front of their television sets with their dinner. I don't care how busy you are—you can take that time with your children."[5]

Instead of watching TV during mealtimes, you can ask your teen questions about his day at school or work. Avoiding complaining about his study habits or criticizing his friends. An ancient proverb says, "Better a dry crust with peace and quiet than a house full of feasting, with strife." Before you raise an issue at the dinner table, you should ask yourself, "Will discussing this matter generate healthy discussion and strengthen family relationships?"

In summary, if you want to develop healthy, caring communication with your teen, you'll have to tackle the communication barriers that keep you from getting through. You won't always win this battle, but when you fail, you can adjust your methods and try again. Is it worth the effort? Keep in mind what better communication can do for you:

- You'll find it easier to communicate about significant issues.
- Your goals will make it easier for you to work toward a stronger, closer relationship.
- Your conversations with your teen will be more satisfying and enjoyable.
- Your self-control will help build peace at home.
- Your investment of time in your teens will pay many dividends: You'll develop a genuine friendship with them and have the opportunity to influence their development into happy, healthy adults.

Action Steps for Five Keys to Communication

- *On the basis of your answers to the four questions at the beginning of the chapter, plan an activity with your teen that will demonstrate your interest and involvement in his life.* Find out— by asking—what your teen's favorite sport, hobby or craft is—and then plan a related activity that will require you to spend at least four hours a week together. Here are some examples of things you could do together:

  - Build a boat or a model airplane
  - Go to a game or a play at their school
  - Shop for some needed outfit or just for the fun of it
  - Invite your teen's favorite teacher or friend's family to your house for an outdoor barbecue
  - Hike a mountain trail or camp out or canoe down a stream
  - Host a pizza party for your teen's friends
  - Give your teen coupons that grant a half hour (or as long as it takes) of your time to hear out any of her concerns

• *Building on the examples in the section entitled, "Develop a Clear Purpose," write out your own purpose or goals for the kind of communication you want with your teen.* Be specific. Discuss your goals with your teen. Ask the following:

"Is this a worthwhile set of goals? Can you suggest others?"

"Do you think it would improve our relationship if I were able to achieve these goals?"

"If I fail on occasion, would you let me know so that I can get back on track?"

• *Make a list of the questions you answered yes to in the section entitled "Avoid Conversation Killers."* Take steps to eliminate these "killers" from your conversations. For example, if you tend to talk longer than a minute without giving your teen a chance to speak, start to time how long you talk. Ask your spouse or teen to help you break these bad habits. Sometimes a discrete signal from your spouse, like a tap on the forehead, can be a great reminder that you've broken your resolution.

• *Think about the last few disputes you had with your teen and isolate moments in each when you wish you had been better able to control your emotional response.* Draw up a plan to improve your self-control. For example, if you sometimes find yourself yelling at your teen, you might decide to fine yourself five dollars (better yet, ten dollars!) every time you raise your voice. Put the proceeds in a special fund that only your teen can use. You'll soon find that the moderate tones of a peaceful family discussion can be just as rewarding and reinforcing.

• *Make a list of words, descriptions, and characterizations that are off-limits during family conversations.* Post the list in a prominent place and then stick to it!

• *Make a list of topics that you think your teen might find interesting.* It could be the prospects for the school's football team, or an article from the paper about an interesting business run by a teenager, or how you feel about some changes going on where you work. Use the list to make your mealtime conversations more interesting. If the conversations are stimulating and fun, your teen will want to come back for more. Carry a 3 x 5 card with you and jot down new ideas as you think of them.

CHAPTER FIVE

THE ART OF SAYING "NO"

Youth today have detestable manners, flout authority, and have no respect for their elders. What kind of awful creatures will they be when they grow up?

— SOCRATES, 399 B.C.

Even before Socrates, the Greek poet Hesiod had written, "I see no hope for the future of our people if they are dependent on the frivolous youth of today, for certainly all youth are reckless beyond words."

In every era, parents have had significant doubts as to how their teens would turn out. These doubts and fears are rooted in real problems, but things may not be quite as bad as Socrates and Hesiod made it out to be. Civilization has survived. The Greeks seem to have done pretty well for themselves. In fact, you and I haven't turned out too badly, either.

Today, parents of teens are concerned about how best to exercise their authority so that their teens turn out at least as well. As I've discussed elsewhere, the central issues of adolescence are created by our teens' need to establish their own identity and independence. This means that authority issues are among the most important, and often the most volatile, that parents and teens must work on.

As the parent of a teenager, you'll quickly discover that the rules that worked when they were younger don't seem to apply any more. Teenagers become increasingly sensitive to the reasons behind your decisions, as well as the ways in which you communicate your decisions to them. Your job is to learn new ways of talking—communication strategies and methods that both fit your teen's new needs and help you accomplish your goals as a parent.

You'll find your communication skills challenged every day. At a parenting seminar, I asked the parents of adolescents to write down their biggest concerns about exercising their authority. Here are a few of their responses:

"Finding consequences that can actually be enforced."

"Being worn out by my teen's complaints about my decisions."

"Being consistent and following through on what I say I'm going to do."

"Coming on too strong, sounding too harsh."

"Agreeing with my husband on what the boundaries should be."

"Fearing arguments. I don't think I have the authority to say no and have it be accepted."

"Saying 'no' too quickly, then feeling the need to change my mind."

"Reacting emotionally without thinking through my response."

"Giving in and giving up too soon."

Do any of these sound familiar? All of these parents have legitimate concerns about how to be an effective parent without either abusing or giving up their authority. And all of their concerns can be traced to underlying problems with their communication styles. Unfortunately, given the broad range of situations you and your teen will encounter, and given the strong feelings that often exist on both sides of discipline issues, it can be difficult to be both consistent and fair, and to promote effective communication with your teenager.

The best way to find your way through this perplexing array of decisions, discussions, disagreements, and compromises is to establish a few basic principles that you can apply every day. Throughout my counseling of parents and their teens, I've discovered six fundamental rules that seem to help parents when they need to exercise their authority. These six principles are easy to remember and broad enough to be useful in a wide variety of situations. You'll find that they help you keep the lines of communication open, avoid the mistakes that can disrupt your relationship with your teen, and increase the chances that you'll make smart, practical choices.

Principle 1: Show Your Teen That You Make Decisions Based on Goals

As I noted in chapter 3, one of the best ways to build better communication with your teen is to have clear goals in mind when you talk to him. The same holds true for decision making. Unless you base your decisions on standards, your choices will seem confused, inconsistent, and arbitrary.

For example, I find the following goal helps me decide how to deal with my children:

I want to train my children how to make wise decisions and take full responsibility for their choices.

Let's test this goal. For each of the following list of actions, answer the question, "Will this action help me reach the parenting goal above?" Write "yes" or "no" in front of each item.

_____ 1. Setting out your teen's clothes for the next day.

_____ 2. Waking your teen up every morning.

_____ 3. Making job interview appointments for your teen.

_____ 4. Saying, "Do this because I said so," to your teen.

_____ 5. If your teen oversleeps and is late for school, suggesting that she tell her teachers she's sick, instead of admitting the truth so she won't get marked down for missing a day.

_____ 6. Asking your teen for help solving a problem you have at work.

_____ 7. Asking your teen what she'd do if someone tried to sell her a term paper to turn in as her own.

_____ 8. Asking your teen what the consequences of a given action would be.

_____ 9. Exploring alternative solutions to a problem, and the long-range consequences, with your teen.

_____ 10. Saying no, giving your reasons, and remaining firm about an action that you find unacceptable.

As you can see, the correct course of action often becomes clear instantly when your choices can be measured against a goal.

Having a goal in mind makes it much easier to avoid the inconsistencies and uncertainties that teens perceive as unfair.

When you set goals for your teen's development, it's important that you share them with your teen. He needs to understand what your expectations are, and the reasons behind your decisions. You need to show him that you appreciate his natural drive for autonomy—that you want him to become a fully functioning, mature adult, and that your decisions are aimed at helping him gain his independence.

For some teens, the shift from dependence to independence can't happen fast enough. They may need help to see the long view, to notice that they really are making progress toward adulthood. Discussing your long-range goals, and how you're applying them to their current circumstances, can help them see the big picture. It can help them be more patient with the limits and compromises that you're asking them to accept.

For example, when Jud turned sixteen, I told him I was pleased to see that he was taking more—and that I could take less—responsibility for his behavior. He had just received his driver's license and was going to be allowed to drive our car on his own—a new privilege made possible by his demonstrating a new level of maturity and independence. I told him he had earned it.

Then I showed him this simple diagram:

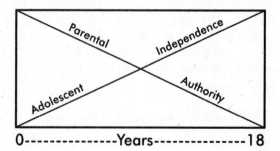

Jud's comment was, "Dad, that's not exactly right. The lines of authority and independence are never straight. They go up and down. Freedom is not given evenly through adolescence. Sometimes a parent gives freedom and then needs to take it away." He's right. There is a lot of give and take in the testing of and earning of privileges and responsibilities. We decided that the graph might still be useful for showing the general direction of the shifting of authority and independence between parent and teen.

It's also clear that we can expect more conflict and confusion than usual at points where the lines of parental authority and teenager independence intersect. This is a perfectly understandable and totally predictable outcome. You will learn to anticipate these moments of greatest conflict as you track your teen's growing independence. It helps to remember that this transfer of control is both inevitable and healthy.

During this transition, your parental role shifts—from being a decision maker for your teen, to being more of a consultant.

Parental Decision Maker (Childhood and early teens)	**Parental Consultant** (Late teens)
1. Makes most decisions	1. Guides decisions
2. Bears major responsibility	2. Shares responsibility
3. Has control	3. Has influence
4. Acts on information	4. Provides information

Making decisions based on long-term goals is really a three-stage process: first, clarifying your own goals; second, learning to apply these goals to specific situations as they arise; and third, helping your teen see the long-range implications of the decisions you're making.

The real key is sharing your goals with your teen. Explain the long-range payoffs *for her* enthusiastically, so that your teenager knows that your rules and regulations are not arbitrary, mean, or meaningless, but are designed to bring her to full maturity and independence as an adult.

Principle 2: Strengthen Your Relationship Power

When parents have any kind of authority or influence in their children's lives, it's because their children understand that parents have real power over them. Basically, there are four kinds of parental power:

1. Physical   (Your superior strength)
2. Intellectual   (Your superior ability to reason)
3. Material   (Your ability to give or withhold things)
4. Relational   (Your personal influence)

Early in your child's life, you may have to use physical force, reasoning, or rewards as your principle forms of power. In the long run, though, there is no way you can win a power struggle with your child by these means. By the time your children are teens, your most effective form of parental power is the strength of the relationship you have with them.

With relational power, you influence your teen through the personal esteem he has for you, rather than through fear or intimidation. This kind of influence is much better than the other three forms of power, because your teen will respect it and respond to it even when you're not around. If you have a strong relationship with your teen, he'll follow your rules because he respects your authority, not just because someone is watching him. In the long run, it's the only approach that has a lasting influence with teens. How else can a 110-pound mother get her 175-pound son to take out the garbage or come home at a decent hour?

Relational power is built through the principles of caring communication discussed in chapter 2. You build it by listening intently, by looking at your teen's side of the issues as well as your own, by spending time with her, by letting her know you love her. You cannot build relational power by letting your teen do whatever she likes. Relationship power, like the caring communication it's based on, is firm and decisive. You are still responsible for enforcing discipline if and when necessary. However, building relationship power means that you can't use threats, insults, yelling, and physical force to get your teens to do what you want. Building your influence with your teens will give you all the "pull" you need to achieve your parenting goals.

Principle 3: Develop a More Democratic Parenting Style

On the basis of a careful study, researcher Diana Baumrind has identified three styles of parental discipline and demonstrated how each pattern shapes the child in a different way.[1]

Autocratic parents favor punitive or forceful methods to curb their child's behavior. They discourage negotiation or verbal give-and-take because they expect their children to believe that parents are always right. The autocratic approach to discipline is more closely related to a parent's feelings than to his thoughts or beliefs. It reflects a parent's reaction to stress and frustration more than his long-term parental goals.

According to another study of 7,050 high school youth by Strommen and Strommen, this kind of parental over-control lowered teenagers' self-esteem and created strong feelings of self-condemnation. The study indicated that adolescents living under autocratic parents were likely to exhibit the following behaviors: hostility toward their parents, antisocial activities, feelings of social alienation, rejection of traditional moral standards, and the inability to relate well to people.[2]

Permissive parents think of themselves as resources to be used as the child wishes—not as involved mothers and fathers responsible for shaping the child's future behavior. They want their children to feel free of restraints and to develop as they choose. However, many teens perceive this kind of permissiveness as a form of rejection. They may feel that their parents really don't care about them. Said one teenager in California,

"Why does it always have to be my decision? Why can't my dad just say, 'You can't go'? I think that if somebody really loves you, they don't just let you do whatever you want."[3]

According to Strommen and Strommen, adolescents with permissive parents display one or more of the following characteristics: they are unlikely to go out of their way to help people, less willing to live by the moral standards of their parents, more likely to become involved in the use and abuse of alcohol, sex, and drugs, less likely to relate well to others, and less likely to be religiously and ethically motivated.[4]

Democratic—or *authoritative*—parents combine firm authority with a healthy amount of flexibility and freedom in their approach to parenting, especially as teens get older. In the sense we're using it here, the word "democracy" doesn't have much to do with politics. The democratic parent affirms a child's unique personality and way of approaching things, but at the same time holds the child accountable to their standards for behavior, attitudes, conversation, and the quality of their relationship.

Democratic parents give their children an opportunity to talk over rules that they do not like or understand. As a result of their discussions, parents may modify the rules if they feel there is good reason to do so, or decide to preserve them as is. In any case, democratic parents do not let their children decide what the rules are and whether and when to enforce them.

On the basis of her research of preschool children, Baumrind concludes that authoritative or democratic parents give their children a better chance at becoming happy, healthy adults than do autocratic or permissive parents.[5] The Strommens came to the same conclusion on the basis of their study of young adolescents. They found the children of democratic parents to be more service-oriented, more concerned about people, free from feelings of alienation, and more committed to a religious faith.[6]

A striking illustration of the contrasting effects of these different styles of discipline is seen in a study of the use of marijuana by college students. The findings showed high use of marijuana by students of permissive parents, medium use by students who viewed their parents as autocratic, and low use by students who viewed their parents as democratic. Apparently, the strength of the parent-child relationship and the parents' willingness to listen to and respect their child's opinions play key roles in whether a teenager adopts his parent's values.[7]

If your parenting style has been more autocratic or permissive than authoritative in the past, you should begin to try to change your approach now. Don't blame yourself for your mistakes, or feel like it's impossible to change. The past is over and done with. Now, in the present, you can ask your teen for forgiveness for the way that your parenting style has hurt your relationship, and choose to work at developing a more effective style in the days ahead.

Principle 4: *Apply Discipline with Respect*

The literature of parenting is crowded with methods for disciplining the uncooperative or disobedient child. With older children, the techniques depend almost entirely on communication. Teenagers are old enough to know what their parents expect, what the limits of appropriate behavior are, and how to go about applying family rules in different situations. *How* you communicate your rules, and how you apply discipline, can make all the difference in the world to the effectiveness of your attempts.

Most parents would agree that their teenagers still need discipline, but many of them confuse discipline with punishment. These two words actually describe very different approaches to dealing with undesirable behaviors.

Punishment involves trying to change a teen's behavior through words or actions that are angry, punitive, insensitive, or insulting. Discipline, on the other hand, involves words and actions designed to instruct, train, and correct. The word "discipline" comes from the same root word as "disciple," which means "learner." Discipline describes a more positive use of parental authority that can help the adolescent learn appropriate behavior.

Psychologist Bruce Narramore, in his book, *Adolescence Is Not an Illness*, shows the difference between discipline and punishment in a way that I find very helpful.[8]

	Punishment	Discipline
Purpose	Justice, or to inflict penalty for an offense	Promote maturity and growth
Focus	Past misdeeds	Future correct attitudes and actions
Attitude of Parent Figure	Anger	Love
Resulting Behavior	Conformity or rebellion	Growth
Resulting Emotion	Fear, guilt, or anger	Love and security

Let's apply this concept of discipline to the following situation.

Situation: A teenager comes home an hour after he's due, even though parent and teen have discussed why it is important to respect the curfew.

Punishment Approach

Parent: (with anger) You're really in trouble now! I told you to be home an hour ago! You're grounded for the next month!
Teen: But Dad, I was …
Parent: (yelling) You were late! One whole hour late!
Teen: But I can explain …
Parent: I don't want to hear it! You always seem to make up a story. You can't handle responsibility. You don't even know how to come home on time.
Teen: (yelling back) That's not fair! Were you ever late? Did you ever make a mistake? Would you ever admit it if you did?

Discipline Approach

Parent: (firmly) Son, what happened?
Teen: Dad, we went out to get something to eat after the game and I just lost track of the time.
Parent: I can understand how that can happen. But we had a firm agreement. I feel somewhat betrayed when our agreements are broken.
Teen: I know, Dad. I'm sorry.
Parent: I forgive you, son. Since this is not the first time this has happened, there will be a consequence. You will be grounded for a week as a reminder of the importance of our agreement.

Comment: Taking the punishment approach creates little real communication. The father's anger produces more anger, defensiveness, and sarcasm in the teenager, and a real strain on the relationship. Additionally, the teenager has little incentive to try to make positive changes. Taking the disciplinary approach, the father withholds his judgment, asks for more information, keeps communication going on an objective, rational level, discloses his own feelings, draws upon his relationship power to exert his authority, and explains his disciplinary response in a way that is much more likely to give his teen the motivation to change for the better.

Parents will readily admit that getting their teen to obey the rules is easy when they're around, and much more difficult when they're not. Real discipline, based on firmness and caring communication, is the only kind that will help the teenager learn to follow the rules even when their parents aren't present.

It's easy to fall into the trap of yelling and screaming at misbehaving or disobedient teenagers as a way of releasing your frustration and anger. Some parents rationalize verbally abusing their teens on the grounds that, "It's the only language they understand."

Even when they are being masterfully obnoxious, our teens are not always the real source of our emotional outbursts. Often, our own past failures, our frustrations of the day, our worries about tomorrow, or our discouragement over not reaching our expectations are behind these responses. There's no way to escape all of our problems, but it is possible to use them as opportunities for a fresh start. I like the way Stephen Covey put it in *The 7 Habits of Highly Effective People*: "The proactive approach to a mistake is to acknowledge it instantly, correct and learn from it. This literally turns a failure into success. 'Success,' said IBM founder T. J. Watson, 'is on the far side of failure.'"[9]

Principle 5: *Learn to Say No Calmly*

"Okay," you say, "I'll try again. But how do I stay calm when I have to say no to my teen and my teen starts yelling at me? How do I stay calm when everyone around me is angry, and I am made to feel that I'm the reason everyone is upset?"

These are fair questions. In order to handle this kind of vocal resistance to your authority, you'll need to learn how to say no calmly. Putting this final principle into action involves learning a new set of techniques for responding to challenges without raising the level of tension in the situation. Once you've read about and practiced these methods, you'll find that you're able to apply them without a great deal of conscious thought—which is especially helpful in stressful moments.

• *Deal with principle, not pressure.* It takes time and effort to clarify your values and goals, but once you've established them, it's much easier to make decisions. Do not give in to pressure to change decisions you've made based on principles. If you do, you'll teach your teen that they can get their way by increasing the pressure until you give in.

For example, let's say that one of your rules is that your daughter cannot go on single dates until she is sixteen. Start discussing the rule with her even before adolescence. Discuss her alternatives—such as double dating and group dating. Explain how you've arrived at the rule—how it fits with your goals and values—and why you'll stick to it. Let her know that you are not afraid to say no on principle, and that you will not yield to pressure. By taking this approach, you'll also teach her a valuable lesson on resisting pressure from others.

• *Practice your calm responses.* It might not seem natural to you to respond calmly. You might view each argument or opinion your teen offers as a challenge to your authority. And your teen might seem to listen to you more attentively when you yell in response. But is this the way you want to teach your teen to respond?

If you want to learn how to respond calmly, start practicing calm responses to issues or situations in which you've failed to respond calmly in the past. Explain to your teen that you're changing the way you respond to his or her challenges. Let them know that it would be a mistake to interpret your new calmness as indecision or ambivalence. Draw up a list of different ways to say no, and then practice delivering the lines calmly. For example:

> "I have decided the answer is no. Don't try to pressure me, because I'm not going to change my mind."
>
> "I know this is important to you. I would say yes if I could, but I can't. The answer is no."
>
> "It might be true that all the other boys your age are drinking. But you're not "all the other boys." We've discussed this issue before, and for the same reasons, the answer is still no."
>
> "I am willing to negotiate with you when I can. But this is not one of those times. The answer is no."

"Right now I am very tired and frustrated. I will explain my reasons for saying no after I get some rest."

Saying no calmly works. It trains your teen to take his or her responsibilities seriously—because you do. It strengthens your relationship with your teen because it tells her that you will stand up for something you believe in. It can help you impose discipline—leaving your teen with self-respect.

• *Use the "no sandwich."* Saying no clearly and decisively, but sandwiching it between two positive statements, can help soften the impact. This cushioning is important, because your teen often hears your no as a rejection of him personally, or as a challenge to his "rights." The first positive statement should acknowledge that you really heard what your teen said or asked. This stops him from assuming that your no meant that you misunderstood him. Follow it with a clear and direct no, explaining why you will not or cannot comply with his wishes. Then add another positive statement about something you will do or can say that will ease the sting of your refusal. For example:

"No" Sandwich #1
"I know that you want me to agree with you."
"But I see the issue from a different point of view."
"I acknowledge your right to your point of view and I hope you will acknowledge that I have the same right."

"No" Sandwich #2
"I understand that you want to borrow the Buick for your date Friday night."
"But I need to use the car that night for a meeting that I have downtown."
"I will be happy to let you drive the Ford. You can use the Buick next Friday if you give me enough advance notice."

"No" Sandwich #3
"I understand that you want to go to the party at Pete's house."
"But my answer is no because we both know that there have been drugs at other parties that Pete has had."
"I would be happy for you to have a party for your friends at our house. I'll help you prepare the food if you like."

Your teen is much more likely to accept your decision if they are clear on your reasoning and understand that you haven't made the decision lightly or arbitrarily. Your effort to present it in a positive light should at the very least minimize your teen's hurt feelings and short-circuit any angry reaction.

• *Try the "broken record" technique.* If you've tried the no sandwich and your teen persists in trying to get you to change your mind, your last resort is the "broken record." Stay relaxed and simply repeat "no" or a one-sentence refusal in a calm but firm voice—until the message gets through. For example, you could repeat, "I've made my decision. For the reasons I've stated, you cannot go to the party." Since you don't need to generate new replies with this technique, you can concentrate on keeping your voice firm and calm. Don't reply with sarcasm or a disgusted or hurt tone of voice. If you do, your teen will not only feel disappointed but will get the feeling that he's being attacked. Stick to the decision at hand and don't let the issue be diverted into new arguments.

Principle 6: Get into the Habit of Saying Yes

You should never let saying no become a habit. Whenever possible, you need to give your teens votes of confidence, let them test their independence, try their wings—even if it means they'll fail.

My wife and I try to say yes to anything that will help build healthy self-esteem in our children. We want them to be psychologically strong, to believe that they have inherent value and dignity—whatever anyone else may tell them. We want them to believe that they can do their work well and that they have the capacity to achieve their own personal goals.

We say yes to their growing ability to handle responsibility. We actively work at encouraging our children to develop an inner discipline rather than merely conforming to external controls.

We say yes to their desire to relate skillfully to other people. We want our children to feel comfortable with their peers and with adults. We talk about what attitudes and behaviors are required to develop these skills and try to model them as best we can. We talk about our own mistakes in this area and try to find ways to correct them.

We say yes to our children's right to say no. We want them to develop the courage to say no to anyone who tries to pressure them into doing something that they know is wrong. We want them to be able to say no to their own feelings of intimidation, fear, or worthlessness. We want them to know how to say no to lifestyle choices that, however popular or tempting, conflict with what they know to be right and true.

We say yes to their efforts to show kindness, courtesy, and love to other people—even when it costs us time and money.

We say yes to any worthwhile talents or skills they want to develop: piano, banjo, guitar, horseback riding, tennis, riding a unicycle, or running cross-country.

We say yes to forgiving them and forgetting their past mistakes—and hope that they'll say yes to us in return.

We say yes to their need for an adequate foundation for life, their need to develop a world and life view that encompasses the best for them in the physical, social, mental, emotional, moral, and spiritual dimensions of their lives.

Remember, the more you can say yes to your teen, the more credible you'll be when you need to say no.

Action Steps for Increasing Parental Authority

• *Think about your real goals for your teen's long-range development.* Make a list of your top four or five goals. Give your answers serious thought and consideration—you'll be using them as the basis for your decisions. Revise the list until you are satisfied that it represents the direction you want to take as a parent. Then, for each item, complete the following sentence:

"My goal is to. . ."

See how often you can apply items in your list to the decisions you need to make for your teen. Do you feel comfortable using your goals as a basis for decisions? Which goals don't really work in practice? Which decisions do you have to make that don't seem to correspond to any of your goals?

Use this feedback process to refine and add to your list of goals. The more thought you put into it, the more useful the list is likely to be.

• *Make a list of three things you will do this week to build your relational power with your teen.* (These can be fairly common activities. For example, you can attend a sporting event together, go shopping, or go out for a meal. In any case, the activity should be something both you and your teen enjoy.)

You may notice that you'll find an activity that requires you to spend more time with your teen at the end of almost every chapter of this book. There are very few aspects of the parent/teen relationship that won't be helped by spending more time together. Time is the best medicine for the "aches and pains" parents and teens suffer during the adolescent years.

• *Design a plan that will help you develop a more democratic parenting style.* What changes could you make immediately? Which of your rules or personal preferences will have to be changed? Find a parent whom you know fairly well who uses a democratic style—and try to model yourself after his more successful behaviors.

• *Put yourself in your teenager's shoes for a moment.* From the tone of your voice and the words you use, how would you describe the way you come across to your teenager? List three adjectives that describe how your teen might feel.

It might be interesting to ask your teen to check your answers and come up with a few adjectives of their own. Ask yourself whether your style is more likely to reinforce or undermine your relational power with your teen. What are some adjectives you'd like to be identified by? How can you work at changing the way you come across?

• *Practice saying no calmly.* Make a list of the three most common situations in which you need to say no to your teenager. (For example: staying out too late, borrowing the family car, missing schoolwork, and so on). For each, write out a short script that includes both your teen's question and your reply. Next to your response, make a short list of your goals for other attributes of your response—your feelings, your tone of voice, facial expression, posture, and so on. Describe how you would like to act as exactly as possible. Use this description as a reminder of your goals and your methods when you actually face the situation.

• *Practice using the "No Sandwich" technique by working on your responses to sample questions.* For example, how would you respond if your daughter asked you if she could drive the family car alone, even though her driver's permit restricts her to driving only with an adult in the car?

Cushion statement _____.
The No statement _____.
Cushion statement _____.

• *In which of the five areas of development discussed in chapter 2 (Physical, Social, Mental, Emotional, Moral/Spiritual) do you feel your teen needs the most support or affirmation?* What is one thing you can say today that will reinforce your teen's self-esteem in that area? If you're in the middle of making a decision about something your teen wants to try or participate in, try to find a way to say yes to the request—even if only partially or conditionally—so long as if fits within the boundaries of your goals for your teen.

CHAPTER SIX

IMPROVING YOUR LISTENING SKILLS

*The biggest mistake parents make
is that they do not listen to your whole argument
They always have an answer before you're done.*
— CARL, 14

Everyone should be quick to listen, slow to speak ...
— JAMES 1:19

An Irish proverb states, "God gave us two ears and one mouth, so we ought to listen twice as much as we speak." One of our teenagers' greatest needs is for parents who are willing to listen to them, not as children but as human beings. Teenagers need to be able to tell parents their doubts, their dreams, and their bewilderment as they try to discover why they were born, how they should live, and where their future lies.

How well do parents listen? One junior high respondent in our survey summarized the thoughts of many of our teens when she said,

"Parents are wise and understand everything because they were teenagers. But they are also human ... and not good listeners."

Other studies have come to the same conclusion. Even though listening is the part of the communication process that we learn first and use most often,* most parents end up catching themselves saying, "Would you repeat that?" "What did you say your

---

* Listening takes 45 percent of our communication time on the average, speaking 30 percent, reading 16 percent, and writing 9 percent.

name was?" "Did you say I should turn right or left?" and "Huh?" more often than they should.

In my previous book, *The Art of Talking So That People Will Listen*, I asked,

> *Can you name ten people who listen intently to you ... people who can think your thoughts after you, empathize with you, and know what you're trying to say before you put it all into words? Few people can name five. The great majority of people suffer the loneliness of not being able to share their true inner selves with persons who will hear them out and take time to understand.*[1]

Perhaps you wish you had a good friend who could listen this deeply to you ... and maybe you can understand how your own teen would like the same thing. After all, teens are going through one of the most confusing, unstable periods of their lives. Doesn't it make sense that they need someone who can really listen, too? Being one of your teen's best listeners is probably one of the best ways to ensure that your teen will be willing to talk to you, confide in you, look to you for guidance. You can play that role for your teen, and you can begin by learning how to be a better listener.

How Do You Rate as a Listener?

Learning how to listen well is no big secret. Anyone can become an expert listener if they are willing to take an honest look at their present level of listening skill and take the steps necessary for improvement. Let's take an inventory of your listening skills and try to highlight areas in which you could use some improvement.

First, answer these two critical questions as honestly and objectively as you can:

_____ 1. On a scale of 1 (poor) to 5 (excellent), how would you rate yourself as a listener?

   2. How would the following people rate you on the same scale?

_____   Your boss
_____   Friends
_____   Your spouse
_____   Your teenager

Next, circle the appropriate number from 1 (infrequently) to 5 (frequently) to rate yourself on how often you practice the following good listening habits:

1 2 3 4 5   I maintain direct eye contact.

1 2 3 4 5   I focus my attention on what my teen is saying rather than what I am going to say next.

1 2 3 4 5   I listen for feelings as well as facts.

1 2 3 4 5   I avoid letting my mind wander.

1 2 3 4 5   I tune in instead of tune out on difficult or controversial issues.

1 2 3 4 5   I think first, then respond.

1 2 3 4 5   I think of questions to ask and ask them.

To score yourself, add each of the numbers you circled. Then check your total points against the following:

33-35	Excellent
28-32	Good
13-27	Fair
7-12	Poor

Most people rate their actual listening skills far below their potential for effective listening, which means they understand that they have plenty of room for improvement. Our awareness of this "listening gap" is an important first step toward increasing our listening skills. In this chapter we'll look at why parents don't listen as well as they could, and then focus on how we can make a few slight adjustments in our listening strategies that will produce significant improvements.

"My Teen Won't Talk to Me!"

Sometimes teens will talk for hours to their friends but hardly at all to their parents. The disparity hurts. We may begin to resent our teens' friends, complain that our teens care more about their friends than they do about us, and try in various ways to force them to notice us and pay attention to us. Of course, in almost every case this only makes matters worse.

Teens cannot always make sense of what they are thinking and feeling. Sometimes they fear that if they try to express themselves, it will come out all wrong. They are extremely sensitive to being criticized or laughed at. Not talking turns into a defensive pattern they use to avoid confrontations and embarrassments.

We may be part of the problem. I compiled a list of common complaints from our survey of over eight hundred teenagers. According to these teens, parents commonly:

- Jump to conclusions
- Get angry when we don't immediately comply with their wishes
- Interrupt
- Give the impression they are too busy to be bothered
- Talk too long without giving teens a chance to speak
- Become preoccupied with their own thoughts and feelings
- Fail to ask questions
- Never seem to want to know what teens think
- Don't understand how teens feel

One teen summarized how most teens feel: "If my parents would only stop talking and listen to me for a change, we would get along much better."

You may find it interesting to ask your teen to rate you candidly on the above complaints. In order for this exercise to work, you've got to avoid being defensive or contradicting what your teen says. Just listen. If you're unclear about what something your teen said means, or can't believe what you're hearing, ask questions that will clarify exactly what you have been told. This exercise could be the beginning of a new effort on your part to understand yourself and your teen. You may not pull it off perfectly or immediately, because listening well takes practice and time. Be patient with yourself.

One of the by-products of this exercise is that it shows your teenager that you are interested and are trying to build a better relationship.

Listening versus Hearing

One teen said, "My parents hear me; my friends listen to me."

Another young person said, "My parents say they want me to come to them with problems, but when I do they're too busy or they only half listen and keep on doing what they were doing— like shaving or making a grocery list. If a friend of theirs came over to talk, they'd stop, be polite, and listen."[2]

These comments point to an important difference between hearing and listening. Hearing is a physical process designed to help us get new information. It's only half of listening. Listening is not just physical; it's also psychological. The process of listening helps us understand the thoughts and feelings of the person talking. Listening requires empathy, the psychological capacity to put one's self into another's situation. It requires your full attention.

When we listen well, we don't concentrate on what we are going to say next or criticize what is being said or how it is said. We don't let our teens' tone of voice or appearance block out what they're saying. As good listeners, we don't merely react, which is relatively mindless. Instead, we respond—which is mindful.

One classic way of showing that you are listening instead of just hearing is repeating what another person said, including the feelings behind what they said—to the speaker's satisfaction. Can you remember a time when someone listened to you that well? Do you remember how good it felt?

Effective listening is one of the most powerful relationship-building tools we have. Such listening almost always:

- Conveys genuine interest in what is being said
- Avoids making hasty or incorrect assumptions
- Abstains from making judgmental statements
- Helps the speaker clarify her own thinking
- Leads to solving problems
- Builds self-esteem
- Increases mutual understanding

Imagine how much effective listening would help your relationship with your teenager!

The Qualities of Effective Listeners

The character of the listener is the key to any strategy for good listening. In other words, who we are as persons is more important than any technique, however creative it might be. If we want to listen to our teens in such a way that our teens will talk to us, we will need to demonstrate the following qualities:

Desire. Effective listeners *want* to listen. Most parents do not want to hear arguments, impudence, or belligerence—all common aspects of conversations with teens that can block our best efforts at communication. When I face this kind of problem, my initial response is to give up and blame my son or daughter for the breakdown. Usually, my desire to listen keeps me going. My desire to communicate is what causes me to keep trying to get around the problems.

> *"Jud, I find it hard to listen when you argue with everything I say. I want to listen to what you are saying, but you need to hear me too."*

> *"Jessica, I feel we are not communicating well. Please take a short break from what you are doing and look at me. I want to understand."*

Timing. Effective listeners know *when* to listen. Part of this is trying to anticipate when your teen might be open to talking, but sometimes it also means knowing when the listening task is over. One night as I was working on this manuscript, Jud came bounding downstairs and said: "Dad, I'm reading a book that could have a profound influence on the course of my life ... It's kind of scary." I was so glad that my son wanted to share this big moment in his life with me that I stopped everything, asked some questions, and waited for him to keep talking. But there wasn't any more to be said right then. I think he felt he had been heard and his mind raced back to the process of discovery. I had to wait until later for more details.

Empathy. Effective listeners can tell what the words they hear mean to the speaker. Empathy is one of those words that are tough to define precisely but that everyone understands is a good thing. Empathy means projecting ourselves into our teen's situation and trying to understand what they're going through. Empathy requires that we focus on our teen's feelings and put our own aside for the moment. Empathy requires thinking first and then responding—instead of just reacting. Reacting means saying the first thing that comes to mind. Responding means considering how what we say will affect our teens before we say it. Empathetic listeners can listen with their hearts.

Teen's Statement: I'm not sure I want to go to college. I'm not sure that I can compete.

Reacting	Responding
Parent: Of course you can compete! Why do you think we spent all that money on private schools? That's stupid!	*Parent*: I can understand that. I felt that way too before I went to college. After I got there, I found most of the students were a lot like me.

Self-Control. Effective listeners remember that feelings come and go, that what is said by a teen in a fit of anger probably doesn't represent the teen's real thoughts and feelings. One mother told me that her teen yelled at her, "I hate you!" The mother felt like crying and yelling back something about her daughter's ingratitude. Instead of reacting, she chose to respond—by staying in control of herself and the situation. She said,

> *"Sue, I realize you are very angry at me right now, but it's not okay for you to say that you hate me. I want you to know that when you are ready to talk, I will be ready to listen. Even though I may not agree with you, I care very much about you and how you feel."*

Keeping the channels of communication open is the best way to achieve reconciliation. It's not easy, especially when our teen's language or actions often seem calculated to make us angry, hurt, or upset. It requires a powerful commitment to keep our emotions in check.

Skill. Effective listeners turn good listening into a habit. The best way to become a skilled listener is to practice, practice, practice. You'll find that good listening can be applied in every conversation you have—and that all of your communication will benefit from practicing.

Skilled listeners are fun to talk to, a delight to be around. Even if they are not brilliantly articulate, they know how to bring out the best in anyone who's talking to them.

I like the way someone once described this kind of listening ace:

> *His thoughts were slow, his words were few,*
> *And never formed to glisten.*
> *But he was a joy to all his friends—*
> *You should have heard him listen.*

When we listen that way, our teens will probably want to talk.

ACE Listening Skills

Since listening can become a complex process, it often helps if we have a model or simple plan for the process that we can follow. Here, then, is what I call the ACE Model for becoming an expert listener. ACE stands for Attending, Clarifying, and Evaluating.

Attending means paying attention. This is how we can make sure we're getting the message our teens are communicating. That message includes the speaker's words, facial expressions, gestures, voice tone, volume, and inflection. To sense the message correctly, we need to:

- Look calmly into our teen's eyes (but don't stare)
- Make sure we hear the actual words being said
- Pay attention to body signals, such as downcast eyes, nervous hands, or tense lips
- Eliminate distractions whenever possible (turn off the TV, shut a door, and so on)
- Listen to the speaker's tone of voice

Clarifying helps us get at the meaning of the message. It's normal for us to interpret messages according to our own experience and our mental frame of reference. Unfortunately, since our experiences are likely to be vastly different from those of our teens, this is likely to create a real barrier to communication. In some cases, speaker and listener will end up with a limited match of meanings or no match at all. To me, for example, the word "homework" would naturally include studying for an upcoming test. But when I asked Jud, "Do you have any homework?" he said "No," even though he had three tests the next day. To Jud, studying for a test is not the same as doing the homework that's been assigned.

To find out whether our teens mean what we think they mean, we can paraphrase and repeat back to them what we think we heard them say, along the lines of, "So what you're saying is ... Right?" Here are some additional examples of clarifying responses:

"Can you give me an example of what you mean?"
"How do you feel about what happened?"
"What do you mean by _____? How would you define that word?"

"If you take this action, what might be the consequences?"
"Is this idea consistent with what you said before?"
"What is the purpose of this activity?"
"How important is this to you on a scale of 1 to 10?"
"What is your reason for saying (or doing) this?"
"Do you think this is the right thing to do?"
"What else can you tell me about this that will help me under-
stand?"

The beauty of asking questions like these is that we not only increase our understanding, we also help our teens to clarify their own messages, hear the implications of what they've said, and perhaps come to a wiser conclusion—or perhaps just a better idea of how their statements are coming across.

Evaluating is the stage where we mentally reflect on the infor-mation we have gathered and decide how we will respond. Here it is important to consider several options. For example, we can:

- Ask for more information
- Remain silent
- Express our feelings
- State our opinions

We need to ask ourselves, before we respond to our teen's statement, "Which of the several options I have for responding to my teen will produce the most effective communication?" The key is to make our response a conscious choice on our part—rather than an emotional, knee-jerk reaction.

The three steps of the ACE Model may seem unwieldy and even a little artificial at first. Still, if you're interested in getting more out of your conversations with your teen, it's an invaluable way to make the process work better. It might seem as if it would take a great deal of time to work through the process, but in prac-tice, it helps you understand your teen right from the start.

Applying the ACE Model

ACE skills generate more positive and more valuable com-munication by encouraging our teens to talk to us further. Look at the following example of negative and positive responses, and think about which is more likely to keep the lines of com-munication open:

Negative Responses

"Did you fail your test again today?"

"You think that's bad! When I was young…"

"You're out of your mind."

"You're just getting yourself worked up."

"You'll get over it."

"I've heard enough."

ACE Responses

"How did things go in school today?"

"Tell me more about it."

"That's a new idea."

"This seems important to you."

"You must have felt frustrated."

"I'd like to hear more."

Suppose your thirteen-year-old daughter came to you and announced, "Dad, I've decided to go steady with Freddie." Some messages may go in one ear and out the other, but not this one. You're disturbed. The message makes no sense, as far as you're concerned, because your daughter is far too young to go "steady" *as you understand the word.* You decide to apply the ACE model of listening. The difference between positive and negative responses to your daughter's statement might look like this:

Teen's Statement: Dad, I've decided to go steady with Freddie.

Negative Response

You: You're too young to go steady!

Teen: No I'm not! All my friends are going steady.

You: I don't care about your friends!

Teen: You don't care about my friends? How could you say such a terrible thing?

You: I mean what your friends do is their business. You're not going steady!

Teen: You can't do anything about it!

You: Oh yes I can! You are grounded for the next two weeks!

Positive Response

You: Go steady? What does it mean to you to go steady?

Teen: Oh, you know, just being friends until another friend comes along.

You: When I was young, "going steady" was what you did just before you became engaged.

Teen: Well, it doesn't mean that now. It would be stupid even to think about getting engaged.

You: I agree with that. Tell me more about this lucky guy Freddie.

At best, this is how the ACE model works. Take a few seconds to identify the ACE elements in the positive approach—and the mistakes in the negative approach. Can you sense the value of the positive response—its potential for helping you avoid serious misunderstandings in your conversations with your teenager? And it really is not difficult or time-consuming. Once you get the basic steps set in your mind, you'll find that the thinking process needed to apply the model can happen within a second or two—quickly enough for it to be used in normal conversation.

The model was designed on the assumption that our teens are worth the effort necessary to get to know them, that their feelings and experiences are important to us, that we care about their well-being. If you give it a chance, you might be surprised to find out just how wonderful your teen really is.

When Teens Still Won't Talk

It may be that reading this chapter has made you feel guilty for not listening better. When you compare your performance to the standards we've discussed, perhaps you've realized you don't measure up very well. In fact, none of us do—without constantly making an effort. And we can all improve.

One way to break down listening barriers is to admit our shortcomings to ourselves and our teens. For example, you could say to your teen:

> In the past I have tuned you out. I'm really sorry. Will you forgive me? I want to do much better. If there are times when you feel that I'm not listening, please let me know. I won't hold what you say against you. I really want to know.

Suppose that after trying all this your teen still won't talk to you. Keep in mind that you as a parent can do only so much. At some point teens—adults-in-progress that they are—must take responsibility for holding up their end of the process.

Teenagers seem to go through a stage when their answer to every question is a grunt. It's important to keep in mind that this stage is almost sure to be as unhappy and frustrating a time for them as it is for us. For most teens this is a temporary thing, but while it's going on, nothing seems to work. Even an expert communicator can't get them to talk if they don't want to. If you have taken the steps recommended in this chapter and get no response, don't give up! If you persevere, your teen will not only talk to you (eventually ...) but will want to learn to listen as well. One sixteen-year-old in Florida wrote to us,

"The one message I want to tell my mother is that I love her and that I'm here too if she needs to talk to someone."

Action Steps for Improving Your Listening Skills

• *Take another look at how you rated yourself as a listener in the first section of this chapter.* Choose the areas in which you most want to improve and draft a short list of strategies: "In order to improve my ability to _____, I will ..." If you want to make sure you don't forget or ignore your choices, post the list in a prominent place where both you and your teen can keep track of your progress.

• *After reading the section on why teens don't talk, reflect on the reasons your teen may be reluctant to talk.* Then fill in this chart according to your honest assessment of the problem. This kind of objective assessment can be a giant step toward the solution.

Reason for Not Talking	Strategies Worth Trying
a.	a.
b.	b.
c.	c.

• *Which of the three ACE listening skills (Attending, Clarifying, Evaluating) do you feel you need to strengthen most?* For example, can you think of times when you didn't pay full attention to the message (including the gestural, tonal, and verbal aspects) sent by your teen?_____

How often do you ask clarifying questions to gain understanding?_____

Do you habitually evaluate how what you want to say will affect the quality of the communication before you respond?_____

Pick out specific situations in which you'll try to work on your weak spots during the coming week—and write out what you'll try to change about what you'll say or how you'll act.

• *How would you respond if your teen said, "I don't think I'll ever get married!"* Fill in the space below with positive responses that reflect your desire to listen; then write what you think your teen's response might be. I'll fill in the dialogue for the negative reactions.

Teen's Statement: I don't think I'll ever get married!

Negative Reactions
Parent: That's ridiculous!
Teen: No it's not! A lot of people never get married!
Parent: You're too young to know what you think!

Positive Responses
Parent: _____
Teen: _____
Parent: _____

• *Which of the qualities of effective listeners (Desire, Timing, Empathy, Self-Control, and Skill) do you feel you need to develop?* Decide what you will *do this week* to strengthen your effective listening qualities. Set some goals—with tangible, quantifiable results—and tell your teen your plan. At the end of the week, ask your teen whether he or she has noticed any difference in the way you listen.

CHAPTER SEVEN

KEEPING YOUR COOL IN DIFFICULT SITUATIONS

*When my parents and I get mad at each other
there is yelling, slapping, and "going wild."*
— JENNIFER, 14

Although statistics show an alarming increase in the number of relationships that have suffered from physical abuse, verbal abuse is even more prevalent and can sometimes inflict greater pain. Who can count the damaged emotions and the broken relationships that are the result of hurtful statements and emotions gone wild?

In our survey of parent/teen communication, we asked eight hundred teenagers what happens when they and their parents become angry with each other. Here's a sample of their responses:

"My mom will go over her list of my faults. Sometimes she yells and says she's not yelling."
— JOHN, 12

"We just yell at each other. Then I run to my room, slam the door, and blast my radio."
— NANCY, 12

"I yell at them and try to win the argument. Usually I lose."
— JAN, 15

"When my mom and I argue, we usually just yell at each other and then go into our rooms. But eventually we make up because it affects me very much when the two of us just fight."
— GUY, 16

"My dad usually lectures me."
— TOM, 13

"Dad will start yelling at whoever gets in his way. Mom gets all mushy about everything."
— GINGER, 13

"There is some yelling, some talking back, and a lot of walking away."
— ROBERT, 13

"I get yelled at and then I get in trouble for yelling."
— CINDY, 15

"My mom kind of gets tired and stares. My dad raises his voice and sighs."
— ROBIN, 13

Most parents aren't trained to respond to strong words and feelings. We are often baffled by the intensity and the unpredictability of our teen's emotional outbursts, and perhaps equally so at our own responses—our angry reactions and ineffective attempts to regain control.

It's not easy to respond calmly. Most people need a clear, simple plan that is easy to remember, even in the heat of an emotional confrontation. I'd like to introduce you to one technique that makes it possible to communicate despite strong emotions. I'll use the word CALMLY as an acronym to make it easy for you to remember the six points of the plan:

Control Your Responses
Avoid Vicious Cycles
Listen to Your Teen's Perspective
Motivate Reconciliation
Learn Verbal Self-Defense
Yield When Your Teen Is Right

C = Control Your Responses

We are a nation of shouters. When asked what happens when emotions get hot in the home, one seventh grader quipped, "Let the yelling begin!" More than 70 percent of the teenagers in our survey complained that their parents yell at them. Some parents admit that in the heat of the moment their feelings get the best of them. They claim that there's usually a good reason for screaming ("It's his fault!" or "She made me mad!") and that "the words just come out." Is there some mysterious force that makes us say things in a way we can't control?

Modern psychology has convinced most people that the human personality includes an uncontrollable part (the "id," the primal "beast") that screams for release. So we have been encouraged to holler when we feel like it, say what's on our mind, and "let it all hang out." It's supposed to make us feel better. It will clear the air. It will release pent-up emotional energy. It's good for us, they say.

I'm not convinced. While there are positive uses of anger and healthy, even loud, expressions of it, in all of my counseling experience I have never seen a relationship between a husband and wife or parents and children that was *helped* by yelling. Quite the contrary. I can't imagine anyone listening harder or hearing better because they were yelled at. Yelling attacks relationships, entrenches positions, provokes wrath, and kills dialogue.

The problem is not with rip-roaring debate or argument. It's not wrong to disagree vocally or express strong feelings about a matter. Problems occur when expressing your feelings gets precedence over your respect for another's feelings—and the expression becomes destructive.

I believe we can learn to control our emotions. Feelings are subject to thoughts and thoughts are subject to choice. In her highly acclaimed book *Anger: The Misunderstood Emotion*, social psychologist Carol Tavris writes, "Self-control, especially self-control in the pursuit of emotional restraint, is a human choice, beyond the limitations of instinct."[1]

When we notice feelings such as anger, frustration, hurt, insecurity, bitterness, envy, or revenge, we must train ourselves to choose our words carefully. When we think about what we really want to say and the emotional effect we want our words to have, we increase the chances that we'll be able to make a constructive response.

Sample Response to a Strong Emotion

Sue: I am old enough to do what I want. Ted asked me to go to the movie with him and I'm going. I don't care what you say!

Negative Choice

You: No, you're not old enough to do what you want! Listen smarty, I'm still the boss.

Sue: You can't stop me!

You: O yes I can!

Sue: How?

You: Sheer force if that is what it takes!

Sue: I'll climb out the window!

You: If you try it I'll make you wish you never had!

Sue: What would you do?

You: I won't let you back in!

Sue: That's really dumb! First you won't let me out, then you won't let me back in!

Positive Choice

You: Sue, you are old enough to make certain decisions, but I have strong feelings about your going out tonight.

Sue: Why?

You: Because you have a term paper due tomorrow and you wanted my help with one part of it.

Sue: Well, I can just show you what I want you to do and I can type it when I get home.

You: No, Sue. I will not work on it without you here. The term paper is your responsibility, not mine.

Sue: You're impossible! You don't care about my date!

You: I'm sorry it seems that way to you. I do care about you.

Notice that in the negative choice column, the conversation degenerates into threats, name calling, and sarcasm. It is likely that after such an exchange, feelings will be hurt, the relationship jeopardized, and the argument unresolved. In the positive choice example, emotions are still high at the end, but the message has been clearly and directly delivered, and no real damage has occurred. The parent has remained firm, expressed positive regard for the teen, and stayed in control. Positive choices like this don't guarantee a happy ending, but they allow expression and some venting of the strong emotions without damage to the relationship.

A = *Avoid Vicious Cycles*

When we have had "words" with our teens and tempers have flared, we are in a combat danger zone. Some parents counterattack verbally as a way of gaining the advantage or at least "getting even." Our tendency is to become defensive and guarded and focus only on ourselves. Unfortunately, the bumper sticker message "I don't get mad. I get even!" often describes parents' relationships with their own children. The problem is that attack and counterattack can easily become a self-perpetuating, self-fulfilling, destructive element in the relationship. If we want our relationships to be healthy and satisfying, we must avoid these vicious cycles.

Nancy, aged fifteen, describes what happens when she and her father argue:

> "My dad gets mad easily. When he's mad he doesn't want to talk about it. I say, 'Dad, I want to talk about it.' And he says 'No, not now.' And I'll say, 'But Dad, we have got to talk about it now!' Then I'll get mad and start screaming at him because he puts me off. That makes him more mad and he starts yelling at me. Finally I leave and go to my room. It always happens that way."

It doesn't always have to happen that way. Whatever our limitations, however much we have generated endless rounds of arguing in the past, we can avoid the cycle of verbal attack and counterattack.

Strategies for Avoiding Vicious Cycles

Your best chance for succeeding in avoiding the fights, disputes and disruptions is to learn a variety of peace-keeping strategies you can apply in different situations.

• *Look for patterns in the way you fight.* Try to analyze and understand the argumentative pattern. Learn how it develops. Ask yourself, "Who usually initiates the attack? What sets him off? What is he likely to say? How is the other person likely to respond? Who keeps the fight going? How does it escalate to the next round of attack and counterattack?" Try to describe the way it appears to you. For example:

> "My son contradicts everything I say."
> "I get angrier and angrier until finally I start yelling."
> "Both of us feel hurt."
> "He tells me that he'll say what he wants to."
> "I respond with threats."
> "He goes to his room and turns on his stereo."
> "We don't talk to each other for days."

This cycle can be illustrated as follows.

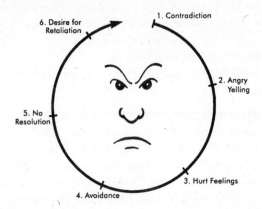

• *Once you've identified destructive cycles, try to break them.* Any vicious cycle requires two or more people. If you know what the pattern is, you can break it by changing the way you respond. You can't control how your teen will respond, but if you can control your first reactions, you do have a number of options that would help to break the cycle.

Sample Response to a Strong Emotion
Teen: You're wrong! You don't know what you're talking about!

Negative Choice	Positive Choice
You: Listen, twit, you failed your last math test. Remember?	*You*: I really do want to understand you, but right now I'm very frustrated. I need to work through my own feelings before I can listen to you the way I want to. Let's talk after supper.

• *Regardless of what you say to break the vicious cycle, you'll need to take the initiative.* Most people find it hard to make the first move, especially if they feel that their kids are being unfair, but it's not impossible. Taking the initiative involves a simple but firm decision on your part to take positive action. Someone's got to take the first step—it might as well be you.

• *If you feel a strong emotional response to an issue, try to delay your reaction.* When you are not clear about how to proceed but you know you're upset or angry, give yourself time to think. Taking the time to decide how to respond will help you control your emotions instead of letting them control you.

Sample Response to a Strong Emotion
A teenager is angry about his parent's unreasonable demands. His parent is angry about the teen's failure to do his chores.

Negative Choice	Positive Choice
You: (Yelling) Don't you dare raise your voice to me! Sit down and shut up!	*You*: Both of us need time to cool off. Let's talk at four o'clock.

Sometimes waiting a few minutes, or even a few seconds, can enable you to choose words and a tone of voice that can stop the cycle rather than perpetuate it.

• *Encourage your teen to talk about feelings.* Not talking about feelings only increases the tension between two people. Encourage your teen to put his feelings into words. Talk about why the feelings are so strong. Try to focus attention not on who's to blame but on how to solve the problem. You and your teen must learn to be expert communicators about your emotions—especially intense ones. It's the only way you'll be able to communicate clearly in difficult situations without damaging the relationship.

Sample Response to a Strong Emotion
A teen's anger about his parent's being late to pick him up at school.

Negative Choice	Positive Choice
You: (Yelling) Get in the car and grow up! Or else you can walk home!	*You*: Jim, yelling is not acceptable. I know you don't like it when I yell at you. And I don't like it when you yell at me. You are angry and maybe you have a right to be. But lower your volume and I promise I'll hear you out.

Commit yourself to staying calm. Refuse to fight anger with anger. My own father and my son think this is the most important strategy. I agree.

Sample Response to a Strong Emotion
The mother is angry at her daughter's failure to do her homework.

Negative Choice
You: What's wrong with you? You're going to fail the whole course! You're grounded for the rest of the month!

Positive Choice
You: I really do want to understand you, but right now I'm very frustrated. I need to work through my own feelings before I can listen to you the way I want to. Let's talk after supper.

Sometimes it's important to remember that we're not the only ones facing difficult or upsetting conversations with people we love. Communication problems in parent/child relationships are probably as old as human language. The book of Proverbs provides several wonderful insights into the need for calmness.

A gentle answer turns away wrath, but a harsh word stirs up anger (Proverbs 15:1).

A hot-tempered person stirs up dissension, but a patient person calms a quarrel (Proverbs 15:18).

A fool gives full vent to his anger, but a wise person keeps himself under control (Proverbs 19:11).

For as churning the milk produces butter, and as twisting the nose produces blood, so stirring up anger produces strife (Proverbs 29:33).

L = Listen to Your Teen's Perspective

What seems to frustrate teens most is when they think their parents are not listening to them. In our survey, Jud and I asked teenagers, "In your opinion, what is the biggest mistake made by parents?"

"Before listening and trying to understand, they yell and then things get worse."
— SAM, 16

"They don't listen to your whole argument. They always answer before you are done."
— BRENT, 14

"Not giving me a chance to express my opinion."
— SHARON, 14

"Not listening to me. Not hearing me out first and then deciding calmly."

— SUSAN, 14

"Forgetting adolescent feelings and thoughts."

— EVA, 15

"Parents don't always let the teenager tell their half of the story. A lot of times they jump to conclusions."

— DOUG, 14

Some parents counter:

"We know what the facts are. Why waste more time?"

"We've heard the same story a hundred times. We're sick of it."

"When my daughter gets all emotional, I just tune her out. She reminds me of my mother."

"When my son feels strongly about something, he gets so dogmatic and arrogant. It drives me up the wall."

Both parents and teens have points. Parents can be downright insensitive and teens can be outright obnoxious, but unless we fully listen to each other's perspective on an issue, we may very well end up arguing about something of no consequence or something we actually agree upon!

I use a very simple illustration to help me remember that I often jump to conclusions about what my son or daughter is thinking and feeling. Suppose someone were to take a tennis ball painted white on one side and black on the other, and hold it up between my son and me. If asked, "What color is it?" I would answer with the color that I see.

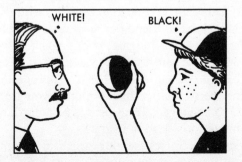

My teen could correctly answer with the opposite color. Neither of us would be able to agree, no matter how long we argued, until the ball was turned and we could see each other's perspective.

I have often wondered how many painful arguments could be avoided if only we made the effort to see how things look from the other's point of view. If we listen well enough to see our teens' perspective, the chances are great that they will reciprocate by trying to understand our point of view.

Strategies for Listening to Your Teen's Perspective

You can learn to listen to your teen's point of view more effectively if you:

• *Accept responsibility for your role in a disagreement.* Since we are older and hopefully more mature, we bear most of the responsibility for building better communication in the relationship. We can't be held responsible for our teens' words, attitudes, or actions, but we are responsible for our responses—our choice of words, tone of voice, body language, and behavior.

• *Work at understanding your teen's feelings.* In a close relationship, feelings are more important than facts. When emotions are high, focus your attention on the feelings your teen is experiencing. You can always ask him to clarify the facts later. Teens will not feel understood until they have adequately expressed how they feel and are convinced that their parents have heard them fully. No lecture will get through, no reconciliation will be accomplished, until the teen's feelings have been fully expressed and understood.

• *Ask questions.* This draws out our teens' thoughts and feelings. Perhaps you have had the experience, as I have, that even you don't understand what you really think and feel until you've had a chance to express yourself to a trusted friend—who will hear you out, let you vent, blow away the chaff, forget the silly parts, and credit you with being smart enough to come up with the right conclusion. That's the kind of friend our teens need us to be.

• *Don't be judgmental.* Judging, as I am using the term, means pronouncing a sentence before all the facts are in. It means responding critically before you know whether it's appropriate. It's being against the other person rather than for him. If you are like the rest of us, you hate to be judged. Teens hate to be judged, too. Judging can stop communication dead in its tracks.

• *Listen carefully.* Sometimes our teens may ask our advice on certain matters, but they really want us to just listen. They want a safe, reliable sounding board. They want someone they can trust with their thoughts and feelings. Therefore, your first response ought to be to listen intently. Instead of immediately offering our opinion on what they've said, you should listen. Use the ACE listening skills discussed in chapter 6 to turn that two-colored tennis ball around, to understand how the issue looks from your teen's perspective.

Warning! Seeing "the other side" is not easy. Unlike the tennis ball illustration, disagreements between parents and teens are never totally black and white. Numerous shades of meaning are involved, and we must try to get as close as possible to the shade they see. When you use the techniques outlined above, however, your focus on understanding your teen will help you learn to be sensitive to your teen's particular needs and desires.

M = Motivate Reconciliation

What happens if we've let our emotions get out of hand and in our anger we've said something that has really hurt our teenagers' feelings?

Strategies alone aren't enough to deal effectively with hurt feelings. If the feeling of being wronged is not dealt with constructively, it can act as a long-term plague on a relationship. It can be a constant source of mistrust and friction.

To lift the quality of parent-teen communication to a level that is relatively free from the effects of past mistakes and hurts, we need to take the initiative, to be the first to bury the hatchet and move toward a reconciliation. We need to ask the greatest healing question: "Will you forgive me for my contribution to the problem?"

When we ask this question, we are not taking all of the blame for the flawed communication. One person is rarely the sole fault of a communication problem between two people. Normally, both have contributed to the problem. The healing question, as stated above, is a powerful tool, because both parties can say it honestly without feeling that they have to bear the blame alone. The process of forgiveness sometimes takes time, but when it is granted, there is an exhilarating feeling of freedom, of being able to start over, unshackled by the past.

Forgiving goes against the grain of our natural tendencies. This is why the greatest healing question has such power. Lewis B. Smedes writes in a helpful book, *Forgive and Forget*, "Forgiving seems almost unnatural. Our sense of fairness tells us people should pay for the wrong they do. But forgiving is love's power to break nature's rule."[2]

Our willingness to ask the greatest healing question can influence the whole complexion of our interactions with our teens. Our communication will become supportive rather than defensive. In the following chart, notice which characteristics produce defensiveness and which convey support.

Quality of Communication

Defensive	Supportive
1. Evaluative—labels statements good or bad.	1. Descriptive—describes ideas without judgment.
2. Control—attempts to control the person or conversation.	2. Mutual—allows equal time for expression.
3. Self-centered—focuses only on one's own perspective.	3. Other-centered—focus is on understanding.
4. Attitude of superiority—condescending to the other person.	4. Attitude of equality—aims at achieving empathy.

One of our basic needs as human beings is the forgiveness and support of at least one person significant to us. If we can offer forgiveness and support to our children, we take a giant step toward responding effectively to strong emotions. They'll be on our side, helping us find solutions to our problems—rather than on the other side of a parent/teen battle.

L = Learn Verbal Self-Defense

Some teens develop a mean streak. They'll say whatever they can to hurt our feelings. The reasons behind their verbal attacks may range from feelings of inferiority to a perverse need to control the world around them. The reason might even be a chemical imbalance. Whatever the cause, they become experts at making their parents squirm.

Parents with mean teens often feel guilty about their teens' behavior and blame themselves. They become more and more compliant in hopes that compliance will solve the problem. They reason that the meanness is just a stage and that by ignoring the problem, it will eventually go away.

Sometimes the problem does go away. But should parents have to endure this kind of pain, even if verbal attacks from teens reflect a temporary stage? Parents are not doormats. They don't need to let their daughters and sons wipe their feet on them or abuse them verbally.

You can learn to defend yourself without having to counter-attack, yell, get revenge, or escalate a verbal war. You simply have to teach your teen that no one—not your business associates, not your neighbors, and not your children—has the right to attack you verbally. You can show her that you won't be intimidated. Your willingness to defend yourself will only add to your authority.

Strategies for Verbal Self-Defense

You can learn to defend yourself against verbal abuse by keeping the following principles in mind:

Take charge. As the parent, you should be in charge, the president of the family "firm." Don't try to prove your superiority by getting into power struggles. If you're not fully convinced of your rights and responsibilities as a parent, your teen will quickly try to take advantage of your ambivalence. Act as if you are in charge and your authority is unquestioned.

Whatever you do, don't shout. Show your strength in a firm but quiet assertiveness, not by yelling or becoming belligerent. Yelling is a sign that you have lost control. It's counterproductive.

Model desirable behavior. Teens tend to do what we do, so it is important to commit ourselves to treating them as we would want to be treated. View any verbal defense that you have to resort to as a teaching tool that your teen can learn from and use when needed in his own interpersonal relationships.

Love yourself. Develop a healthy sense of self-esteem. You have God-given dignity and worth that no one can take from you. Refuse to accept a low opinion of yourself. No one should be able to intimidate you—not even your children. If you have to defend yourself, assert and affirm your worth as a person.

Let's apply these principles to common forms of verbal attack.

Put-downs
Teen: You don't want to make my lunch because you're too lazy!

Ineffective Defense
Parent: I'm not the one who's lazy—you are! You never do anything around here!

Effective Defense
Parent: (Lightly) I wish I had the time to be lazy. The fact is, I have more than I can do in the time I have. (Seriously) I feel put down when you attach a negative label to my request. Let's not do that to each other. I need your help.

Defiance
Teen: I will not take out the garbage! That's Bob's job.

Ineffective Response
Parent: Oh yes you will! You will do what I tell you to do, you ungrateful child!

Effective Response
Parent: (Calmly) Bob is mowing a lawn. Our guests will be here in half an hour. I need your help to get ready for them.

Threats
Teen: I'll show you. I'll leave home and get my own apartment somewhere.

Ineffective Response
Parent: No! Don't do that! You don't know what you are doing! It'll kill me to think of you roaming the streets! What will people say? Okay ... Okay, go ahead and do what you want ... but please come home!

Effective Response
Parent: John, I don't want you to leave. But if you insist on leaving, I can't stop you. I hope you'll reconsider this, and I'd like to keep talking ...

Frustration
Teen: I'm sick and tired of you telling me what to do! I'm sixteen, for heaven's sake! Get off my back!

Ineffective Response
Parent: I'm sick and tired of telling you a hundred times to do what any responsible sixteen-year-old would already have done!

Effective Response
Parent: Kim, I really dislike having to tell you what to do. Yet for this family to function smoothly, some things have to get done that are not being done. How do you suggest we solve this problem?

Y = *Yield When Your Teen Is Right*

Suppose you and your teen have had an argument and that you gradually begin to realize that your teen was right. Let's say you've remembered some new piece of information that came up during the discussion that you had missed before. What can you say? Is it ever right for a parent to yield to a teen? If you do, what happens to your parental authority?

Think about how you felt as a teenager when you knew you were right. How did you feel about your parents when they refused to change their position or refused to listen to your evidence? Did you have more or less respect for them? What did you wish they would do?

I remember feeling a sense of euphoria when my father said, "Son, I think you're right" or "Paul, I guess I made a mistake." Part of the euphoria came from the feeling that I had won a personal victory, that I had shown that even as a teen I had something to say that made sense, that I could talk on an adult level and make valid points. It made me feel very good about myself. But the euphoria also reflected my sense that my father had won a victory, too—a victory over stubborn pride, over having to prove he was always right. He was strong and secure enough to admit his mistakes, and I respected him for it.

If you do realize that you've been wrong, or you realize that you've totally missed the point of something your teen has said, let your teen know about your change of heart as soon as you can. You'll find that not only do they respect your willingness to admit a mistake, but that they'll be much more willing to own up to their own stubbornness in the future. This is a case where both sides can agree to lose the battle, but win the war!

Admitting to a mistake is one of the hardest things an authority figure (that's you!) has to do. My wife and I have realized that we can't always take the necessary steps under our own power. That's why we find ourselves praying prayers like this one by Peter Marshall:

> Lord, when we are wrong, make us willing to change. And when we are right, make us easy to live with.[3]

Action Steps for Responding CALMLY to Strong Emotions

• *Think of some recent conversation with your teen in which you found it difficult to control your responses.* Make a note as to what you think it was that triggered your strong emotions, and write down how you intend to handle a similar situation the next time it occurs.

• *What can you do to avoid the vicious cycles of hurtful remarks that can do so much to damage your relationship with your teen?* Discuss with your teen how the patterns seem to develop. Use the last few arguments you've had as raw material to look for patterns of escalation and revenge. Work out a plan that you both agree will help you communicate more calmly when you are angry with each other. This can include all sorts of conversational tactics—ranging from time limits to taking turns to setting certain comments off limits.

• *What strategies in the section on "Listen to Your Teens' Perspective" do you think would be most helpful in communicating with your teen?* Choose at least one strategy as a goal and write down a specific plan for implementing it today. Pick some quantifiable measures so that you can see whether the plan is working. At the end of the week, ask your teen whether he's noticed a difference in your behavior.

• *If someone asked you the "greatest healing question" ("Will you forgive me for my contribution to the problem?"), how do you think you'd feel?* Think of the last few instances where it might have helped if you had asked the question, and consider what difference it might have made in what happened next. Plan to ask your teen that question whenever there are hurt feelings because of something you said or did. It might help to post the question on your refrigerator or somewhere that you check several times a day as a continual reminder of your plan.

• *Reflect on a recent verbal attack you received from your teen and write it down.* Then script a brief defense that follows the guidelines in the section, "Learn Verbal Self-Defense."

• *Suppose you get in an argument about your teen's watching TV because you assume he has not done his homework.* Later, you discover that you were wrong. Write down what you would say to your teen.

CHAPTER EIGHT

WHAT TO DO WHEN YOU DISAGREE

It's hard to rebel when I know you're trying to understand.

— TIM, AGE 15, TO HIS MOTHER

As part of a few recent seminars I have asked parents to jot down how they acted during their last major conflict with their teenager. Here are some of the typical responses:

"I lost my head and said some mean things."

"I cried."

"I made some irrational demands and grounded my son for a month."

"I slapped my daughter across the face."

"With one word I blew a relationship I had spent years building."

As we discussed in the previous chapter, most parents want to learn how to respond differently. We want alternatives to giving in or getting even. This chapter provides a simple, easy-to-remember plan for resolving conflict that you can use to repattern and rewrite even your worst conflicts.

The Nature of Conflict

Before we can use the Conflict Resolution (CR) model effectively, we need to understand how conflict works in the family. As a quick way of evaluating how you feel about this issue, check whether you agree or disagree with the following statements.

Your Opinion on Conflict

Agree	Disagree	
_____	_____	1. It is sometimes necessary to yell at our teens to get them to do what we want.
_____	_____	2. We must compromise our convictions to maintain peace in the home.
_____	_____	3. Negotiation is to be reserved for adults, not teenagers.
_____	_____	4. If we admit mistakes to our teens, we will lose our authority over them—and their respect.
_____	_____	5. It is better to give in to our teens than to refuse their wishes and make them angry.
_____	_____	6. Everyone knows that it's wrong to get angry.
_____	_____	7. It is better to say whatever comes into our minds than to follow a plan or model for resolving conflict.

Personally, I disagree with all of them!

Learning to resolve conflicts will require us to draw a few careful distinctions. For example, although disagreements between parents and teens are inevitable, it is not true that yelling, hitting, or name calling are also inevitable. In fact, this chapter is built on the conviction that parents and teens need to learn to avoid that level of conflict altogether. Our goal should be to develop a method by which fights can be avoided and conflicts can be resolved calmly.

It is helpful to remember that conflicts between parents and adolescents can have a healthy side. Some conflict seems to be a normal part of growing up. In *Try Being a Teenager*, Earl Wilson explains this kind of conflict as the natural result of the collision between the adolescent's desire for freedom and the parent's need to control.[1]

Control and Freedom in Collision

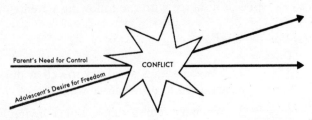

David Augsburger, in *Caring Enough to Confront*, writes,

Conflict is natural, normal, neutral, and sometimes even delightful. It can turn into painful or disastrous ends, but it doesn't need to. Conflict is neither good nor bad, right nor wrong. Conflict simply is. How we view, approach and work through our differences does—to a large extent— determine our whole life pattern.[2]

Maybe conflicts with our teens are not always our fault—or theirs—after all! Maybe if we could look at resolving conflicts more objectively, and work at reducing our fears and the defensiveness we bring to the subject, we'd have more of a chance of successfully resolving our conflicts.

To really understand how conflict works, we'll need to make a basic change in our attitudes *and* learn a new communication skill.

First we'll need to accept that conflict is fairly normal. With teenagers we need to be able to accept an almost daily dose of conflict. We need to learn to expect it, anticipate it, and prepare for it. We cannot allow the fear of conflict to overwhelm us. We need to understand the role that conflict plays in our relationship with our teen before we can begin to manage it.

Second, we will need to develop a model for resolving conflicts that shows us what steps we can take to defuse them. Knowing how conflicts develop as well as the best way to resolve them will make it a little easier for us to relax with our teenager. When we feel as if we understand the process better and are more in control of situations that might lead to conflict, we'll be able to spend more energy on resolving the problems than on just coping with the conflict.

From Revenge to Resolution

Conflicts that degenerate into sharp words and hurt feelings can burn permanent scars into our memories. These out-of-control conflicts provoke two common responses: retreat and revenge. When we retreat, we suppress our feelings, which flare up in other contexts and make ourselves and others miserable. When we take revenge, we set in motion a lose-lose dynamic of blame and counter-blame, attack and counter-attack.

"Why pick on me? What did I do?"
"It's not my fault—it's yours."
"Why did you get us into such a mess?"
"You made me do it!"
"How stupid can you get?"

The Apostle James wrote that the tongue, though small, has great power. Like a spark, it can set a whole forest aflame (James 3:3-6). Both retreat and revenge can escalate the blaze out of control. The only way to avoid this kind of conflagration in parent/teen conflicts is to practice conflict resolution—talking through our disagreements and finding a way to quench the fires of discord.

Conflict resolution requires self-control and an array of conversational skills. For example, we can choose a tone of voice that conveys respect even though we're upset. We can choose not to repress our feelings or cover up a conflict, not to automatically assume all the blame ourselves, or try to fix the blame on another.

We can start by trying to remove the adversarial "us versus them" aspect from our conflicts with our teens. Among the many factors that can cause or contribute to conflict are psychological stress, incorrect assumptions, poor communication, frustrated plans, unrealized dreams, a poor self-image, hormonal imbalances, misunderstandings, fatigue, rejection, too much pressure, or feelings of failure. All of these can be the roots of conflict, or just the influence that sparks a difficult situation into an outright conflict.

Whatever the explanation, once we've moved past the idea of assigning blame for the conflict, we can try to develop ways to resolve it. We need a plan that will help us avoid the same communication traps and failures that we've experienced in the past.

A Model for Conflict Resolution

Sometimes in the heat of an argument, we don't think as clearly as we would like. That's why we need a model for resolving conflict that's easy to remember—one that won't slip our minds even when we're angry or frustrated. The following model lays out a specific series of positive responses that we can follow to take the conflict out of almost any conversation. It can help us turn the destructive communication habits that plague so many parent/teen relationships into new patterns that not only lower the level of conflict in the situation but can help us move toward a resolution. The model describes four steps we should take in each conflict-prone situation.

Steps	Messages
1. Define the problem.	"I hear ..."
2. Look for agreement.	"I agree ..."
3. Try to understand your teen's feelings.	"I understand ..." "I think ..."
4. State your views calmly.	

Especially during those times of impasse, when neither we nor our teenagers seem to make any sense to the other, we will find this Conflict Resolution (CR) model useful. At first, using it may seem forced or mechanical, but with practice it will seem as natural as riding a bike. It will help us to keep our balance and to become adept at talking through conflicts to their resolution. Once you've gotten used to the method and developed some skill in using it, both you and your teen will appreciate the difference it makes in your communication.

The first step is to *define the problem*. In any given conflict with your teen, how often do you really know what the problem is—or whether you've misjudged their motives and intents? How often have you reached the end of your patience, only to realize that you had totally misinterpreted the point your teenager was trying to make?

If you don't bother to establish and agree on the real source of your disagreement, you're likely to misunderstand what your teen is trying to say. After all, few teens are experts on expressing their feelings, and few parents are skilled at listening to their teens. It's important to correct these miscommunications as soon as they occur, or both the conversation and the relationship are bound to deteriorate.

It's easy to see how this destructive process works. Let's say that your teen makes a statement that you, for some reason, misunderstand. You may begin to argue against what you thought he said. Your teen, puzzled by your objections, which (since they're based on a misunderstanding) probably sound arbitrary and unfair, may turn argumentative. His arguments, in turn, may provoke you into an emotional response.

Both of you are confused and upset, and the focus of the conversation has changed from the issues to your emotions. In a matter of seconds, the argument can move hundreds of miles away from the original problem to include all of the running emotional issues that surface in families. Your conflict has nothing to do with the original problem—which may have been very easily to solve, if only you could remember what it was! In the later stages of writing this book with my son, the two of us faced the pressures of much to do and little time in which to do it. I remember one night when this pressure, combined with a few incorrect assumptions, contributed to a major conflict between us.

I complained that Jud was procrastinating. He countered with evidence that proved (to him) that he was working as hard as he could. Further, he felt hurt because he thought that I was questioning his commitment to our project. I felt unhappy because he was angry at me for trying to help. We finally resolved the conflict by redefining the problem. It became clear to both of us that the problem was not Jud's procrastination, as I had assumed, or my questioning his commitment, as Jud had thought. When we defined the real problem behind the conflict—Jud's uncertainty about how to proceed—we took the biggest step toward resolving the conflict.

One way to make sure that you both agree on the real problem is to state your understanding of it as clearly as possible, accompanied by a request for agreement or clarification. This could take one of the following forms:

"What really is our problem?"
"It seems to me that the problem is ... Right?"

Another way is to rephrase or repeat what you think the other person thinks the problem is, and ask whether she agrees with your description of her point of view:

"I hear you saying that ..."
"Are you saying that ...?"

Refuse to move on to new material until you can agree on the problem.

The second step in the process is to *look for agreement*. Normally, you will find several points in your teen's arguments with which you can agree ... if you listen for them. When we acknowledge the areas in which we agree, we limit the scope of the argument, which can make overwhelming problems seem more manageable. This both reduces the tension you feel and turns the focus of the discussion onto a very specific, often resolvable issue.

To express areas of agreement, say, "I agree that ..." and then list details on which you both can honestly agree. For example:

"I agree that I said some harsh words to you. I'm sorry."
"I agree that you tried to get home on time."
"I agree that many of your friends are dating already."
"I agree that the movie is rated PG-13 and you are fourteen."

Finding areas to agree on during an argument requires active listening on our part—and that's part of its strength. As we discussed in chapter 6, one of the most frequent complaints we hear from teenagers is that their parents don't listen to them—especially when an issue looms between them. This simple step serves to narrow the focus of the dispute and let our teens know that we're committed to working with them to resolve it.

Although most teens know that they can't get their way on every issue, they do expect us to listen. When they know we have listened closely enough to recognize where we and they agree, we have sent them a powerful message of respect.

The third step is to work to *understand your teen's feelings*. Few things are more important to our teens than their feelings. If we misunderstand their feelings, they won't be listening when we try to make our points. By making the effort to understand their feelings, we show our respect for what they consider to be the core of their identity. In many cases, all our teens really want is to be genuinely understood. Many conflicts may be resolved just by paying attention to this single step.

One caution: Don't try too hard to understand your teen. Although that sounds contrary to everything I just said, it's important to learn how to strike a balance between paying attention to your teen's feelings and intruding on his sense of privacy. Sometimes teens don't really understand their own feelings, or may not want us to know what they really feel. If you are not sensitive at this point, your attempts at uncovering your teenager's feelings could leave him confused, embarrassed, or angry. However, the benefits of understanding his feelings are worth some risks—if you're willing to proceed in a sensitive manner.

Never say, "I understand exactly how you feel." Instead, say, "I understand that you might feel ..." and then complete the sentence with one word describing the feeling. What seems like a small difference between these two messages is really a big one. The first conveys to our teens that we are making unwarranted assumptions about how they feel. Teens almost always find this offensive. The second message tells them that we genuinely want to understand and will take the time to find out how they really feel.

Complete the sentence "I understand that you might feel ..." with one word that accurately describes a feeling your teen has communicated to you. You might use one of the following:

angry	depressed	worried
troubled	uncertain	elated
defensive	hurt	anxious
upset	vengeful	happy
sad	confident	afraid

Always convey this message with the impression that you are willing to be corrected if wrong. "I understand that you might feel ... Right?" Offering our own perceptions and asking for feedback will encourage our teens to correct us if we are wrong. If we're right about their emotional state, we'll have demonstrated our insight and understanding. If we're wrong, but give them the opportunity to correct us, we'll have demonstrated how committed we are to getting it right. Either way, we've taken a giant step toward resolving the conflict.

The fourth step asks you to *state your views calmly*. Begin by saying, "I think ..." or "The way I see it ..." and then calmly and briefly state your opinion on the issue at hand. The objective here is to help teens see that there is another point of view besides their own, to show them that your role in the disagreement isn't just to correct or criticize them, and to persuade them to work with you toward solving the problem. Here are some examples:

"I think that our getting-off-to-school routine is not working. Somehow we have to stop the yelling and last-minute panic. Neither of us likes it when the other is angry. If we start breakfast at 6:30 A.M., we can make it without undo pressure."

"The way I see it, you're not getting the sleep you need. When you feel exhausted, everything suffers: health, personality, grades. Nothing seems to go right. I think it is reasonable to ask you to be in bed by 11:00 P.M. on school nights."

"Son, I want us to solve this problem together. I would like to give you an opportunity to suggest options that would be acceptable to us both."

Notice the emphasis on calmness. If staying calm isn't your normal reaction to conflict, you may have to develop some new patterns. It's difficult, but it can be done. (Hopefully, you've learned some techniques on how to keep your cool from the discussions in the previous chapter.) If your normal pattern is yelling and screaming, is it working? It may make you feel self-satisfied for a moment, but is it drawing you and your teen together or forcing you apart? Does it help you achieve understanding or destroy it? Does it teach your teen how to deal effectively with her own interpersonal conflicts or does it merely make you feel better because you ventilated your feelings?

When I was discussing this chapter with my son, he said, "Dad, do you know why I don't yell and scream at you? It's because I don't need to. I know you will listen and try to be fair in your response." I'm grateful Jud feels that way, because I *hate* continual conflict. I won't *allow* constant friction to become a way of life in our home. Life is too short, and our relationship as a family is too important.

The key is to remember that neither retreat nor revenge can solve problems. They may temporarily derail difficult conversations, or offer us release from our tensions and anxieties, but the underlying conflicts will smolder and flare up again later. Threats may give me the upper hand with my teen in the short term, but over the long term my teenager will grow angry, defensive, alienated, and uninterested in any kind of continuing relationship. The Conflict Resolution model gives me the structure I need to handle all of the conflicts I face, from the petty aggravations to the potentially explosive problems.

When you choose resolution as your response to conflict, you'll begin to notice a change in the focus of your conversations. Your disagreements will no longer include the whole range of family issues, and they will no longer depend so heavily on personal attacks and counterattacks. Instead, your disputes will focus on narrow, specific, solvable problems, and both sides will concentrate on finding mutually satisfying solutions. We can diagram the shift this way.

Conflict   *Conflict Reso*   *Conflict Resolution*

As this shift in focus occurs, you'll experience a tremendously positive change in the quality of your own communication style.

- You will speak with, not at, your teen.
- You will be less defensive and more open.
- You will be less angry and achieve a better understanding of family and personal issues.

Resolving Common Conflicts

In this section, we'll show how the four-step Conflict Resolution model applies in common conflicts between parents and teenagers, and compare the "discord exchange" (the way conflicts often develop when we have no plan) with the "resolution exchange" (which follows the CR model). Each problem area begins with a conflict-producing statement.

Although the dialogues are necessarily condensed, you are sure to see parallels to your own experiences.

Problem Area: Curfew
Teenager (15): I'll be late getting home tonight. The guys are having a party at Jack's house after the game.

Discord Exchange

Parent: Not tonight. You have to be home by ll:00.

Teen: No way!

Parent: Don't talk back to me! You heard what I said!

Teen: You just don't understand! The problem is that you never listen!

Parent: I understand perfectly!

Resolution Exchange

Parent: What do you mean by late?

Teen: About l:00 ...

Parent: I hear you saying you want to stay out that late, even though curfew on school nights is 11:00 P.M.

Teen: I know, Dad, but I hate to be the first one to leave.

Parent: I agree that it's hard to have to leave first. I understand that you might feel embarrassed ... Right?

Teen: Right.

Parent: I think we need to remember that you've complained about being tired in school the last few days. If the choice is between being embarrassed and having trouble staying awake in school, I'd like to think that you'd prefer to be a little embarrassed. I know it won't be easy, but I'd like you to be home by 11:00 P.M.

Comment: Our natural tendency to follow the "Discord Exchange" is understandable, especially if we're tired, if we've had a hard day, or if we've fought over the same issue before. It's nearly impossible to develop any real understanding of our teen's concerns, and the cycle of mutual recriminations is likely to continue.

The "Resolution Exchange," on the other hand, uncovered a feeling that might seem inconsequential from a parent's point of view but is very important to the teen. It's probably easy for you to remember some incident from your own adolescence when *you* didn't want to be embarrassed in front of your friends. The Conflict Resolution approach, by identifying and acknowledging these underlying feelings, and then firmly stating your standards, is more likely to produce cooperation in our teens.

Problem Area: Chores
Teenager (age 13): I'm going to Judy's house to listen to some records!

Discord Exchange

Parent: Have you done your chores? (with a negative tone of voice).
Teen: I just did!
Parent: Then please fold your clothes.
Teen: Mom, I have plans!
Parent: You can take five minutes to do that for me.
Teen: No! (muttered)
Parent: Go to your room!
Teen: (leaves, slamming door)

Resolution Exchange

Parent: Have you done your chores? (with a positive tone of voice).
Teen: What chores?
Parent: The ones we discussed this morning.
Teen: Well, some of them.
Parent: I hear you saying that you want to go to Judy's, but you haven't completed your chores as we agreed.
Teen: But it's getting late and if I don't go now there won't be any time left.
Parent: I agree that time is a factor. I understand that you might feel frustrated by so much to do and so little time to do it. Right?
Teen: Very!
Parent: I think that if you had started sooner you would have been finished now. True?
Teen: I guess so.
Parent: What you agreed to do will not take long if you hop to it. Let's get it done.
Teen: Okay, Mom.

Comment: This "Discord Exchange" is taken from an actual dialogue a thirteen-year-old girl wrote on one of our surveys.

She feels she has a very good relationship with her parents and says that the one message she most wants to communicate to them is that she loves them. But she also complains that the biggest mistake parents make is not really listening to their kids. The "Resolution Exchange" may take more time, more thought, and more self-control, but it's also more likely to show our teens that we are listening and give us better opportunities to find out what they really want to tell us.

Problem Area: Dating

Teenager (age 14): Mom, Brad asked me to go to a movie with him. I want to go.

Discord Exchange

Parent: Absolutely not. Brad is a creep!

Teen: He is not! All the girls go wild over him.

Parent: He's not your type.

Teen: Yes he is! I like him!

Parent: But I don't! That's final!

Teen: Who asked you? I'm going to run my own life!

Etc., etc.

Resolution Exchange

Parent: I hear you saying that you want to go out with a boy we discussed before.

Teen: I know, Mom, but this is a chance in a lifetime.

Parent: I agree that his picture is handsome.

Teen: All the girls are crazy about him.

Parent: I understand that you might feel excited about this opportunity.

Teen: Yes, I am!

Parent: I think that no matter how nice he looks, we need to hold to our plan for dating. Let's review the plan.

Comment: This is a good example of how to handle a tough situation. Not only are dating issues among the most volatile that a parent can face, but how this one is resolved will have a long-lasting, widespread effect throughout this parent/teen relationship.

Not all disputes will end in agreement after one "cycle" of the CR model. After all, not everyone agrees on what's best for him or her—or on what the rules should be. In this case the parent returns to the underlying principle that her decision was based on. This takes the focus off the immediacy of her daughter's concern, turning the discussion back to an examination of the "house rules," and defuses any criticism of her as arbitrary, autocratic or authoritarian.

The conflict may continue for some time, but the strength of this exchange is that the parent and teen are still talking. When the communication channels remain open, real progress can occur.

Problem Area: Music
Teenager (age 17): (Playing loud rock music)

Discord Exchange	Resolution Exchange
Parent: I hate that music! Turn it off!	*Parent*: Tom, I hear lyrics in that song that are just unacceptable.
Teen: I like it!	*Teen*: I don't listen to the lyrics. I just like the sound.
Parent: I heard it's shock rock.	*Parent*: I agree that this group has a sound that most teenagers would like.
Teen: It's harmless! Everybody listens to it!	*Teen*: It makes me feel great!
Parent: I don't want you to listen to it!	*Parent*: I understand that you might feel happy when you hear that sound. But I'm more concerned about the messages you might be getting from the music without really paying attention to it. Let's listen to the lyrics together and I'll point out what I mean.
Teen: Why not?	
Parent: Turn it off!	

Comment: When a teenager reaches seventeen years of age, the balance of power for determining the direction of his life has already swung over to him. If we engage him in a power struggle, we will lose. Yet there's still a role for parents—still time to influence and direct. Older teens are more capable of reasoning things out than you might think—and will respond to your willingness to treat them like reasonable people.

While they are very much aware of their need for independence, teens also want to know what we think and why we think as we do. If we can share ourselves with them in a collaborative way and reduce the sense that we are telling them what to do, we will often gain a hearing for our point of view.

Throughout this section we've contrasted two different kinds of responses to disagreements between teen and parent. The chart that follow shows how these approaches reveal themselves in our personal style. It should be helpful to see these distinctions outlined—it can help you check on whether your own behavior is more likely to result in discord or open the door to successful resolutions.

Discord/Resolution

Discord Producer	Conflict Resolver (the CR model)
Immediately assumes he knows what the problem is.	Takes the time to discover and define the real problem.
Tries to gain the upper hand and prove that he's right.	Looks for areas of agreement to reduce the threat of conflict and signal a desire to resolve the conflict.
Talks, doesn't listen.	
Allows choices and actions to be dominated by personal feelings.	Listens actively to understand how the other person really feels.
	States own opinions calmly but firmly.

Unfortunately, your conversations and conflicts won't always follow neat structures. You may not always use the words "I hear," "I agree," "I understand," or "I think" or be able to follow all these steps in every conflict. Yet, the CR model can introduce you to the habit of resolving conflict using some or all of the four steps.

No plan can guarantee peace, but having a plan for resolving conflicts peacefully stands a much better chance of succeeding than depending on your wits and off-the-cuff reactions. Like any new skill, using the CR model may not feel comfortable at first. It will take a clear commitment and conscious effort to make it work. The more practice you get with the model, the more powerfully you'll be able to use it to reduce the level of conflict in your own family.

Action Steps for Resolving Conflict

• *Review your answers to the short quiz at the beginning of the chapter.* Have your opinions changed since reading through this chapter? Take a second look at your answers, then jot down how you've changed your mind, and what changes you'd like to make in how you handle conflict.

• *We've looked at three responses to conflict: retreat, revenge, and resolution.* Make a short list of how the resolution response would benefit you, your family, and your teenager. Now make similar lists for the benefits of retreat and revenge. If you're like most people, the latter lists will be much shorter. Does this help clarify the advantage of conflict resolution? You might also make short lists of the costs of each approach. For which of the three approaches is the cost/benefit ratio most attractive?

• *Describe an unresolved conflict you have had with your teenager:*

The conflict was about_____and has continued because _____.

Now write down a "Resolution Exchange" as you imagine it would develop around this conflict if you used the Conflict Resolution expressions "I hear ...," "I agree ...," I understand that you might feel ...," and "I think ...."

Parent/Teen Conflict:

_____.

Parent: I hear_____
Teen: _____
Parent: I agree _____
Teen: _____
Parent: I understand that you might feel _____.
Right?
Teen: _____
Parent: I think _____.

How is this different from the way the actual conversation went? What do you think made the biggest difference in the outcome?

Whenever you anticipate a conflict with your teenager, try to work out this kind of script in advance. Knowing how you'll handle each of the four steps will take your mind off of the process and help you pay attention to what your teen is saying.

• *Keep in mind that this process won't necessarily work the first time you try it.* In practice, you might want to add a fifth step: Step back, think about what might have gone wrong, think of a new and different approach that might resolve the problem, and try, try again. Think of a time when your best efforts at resolving a conflict failed. What would you do differently? Make a short list of specific tactics you could try.

CHAPTER NINE

GETTING TO KNOW YOUR TEENAGER BETTER

Better a patient man than a warrior,
a man who controls his temper than one who takes a city.
— PROVERBS 16:32

Do you have more than one child? Do you remember how you could detect differences in the way each responded to different situations, almost from birth? Maybe one was calm and slept through the night, while another kept you up at all hours. Or one smiled at everyone, even strangers, while the other showed fear of anyone new. These examples illustrate differences in temperament, which means a behavioral style or inborn disposition to act and think and talk in certain ways.

Growing up in a family with five sisters (no brothers!), I had plenty of opportunity to observe a fascinating array of temperaments at work. One sister enjoyed being in charge (she became a schoolteacher). Another found humor in almost everything (she was often the life of any party). Two demonstrated a great deal of patience and interest in other people (one went into nursing, the other counseling). Another loved to organize the house and clean up after everyone (she manages her husband's office).

Although most parents are aware that they and their children have distinct personalities and communication styles, most haven't given much thought to how these styles interact—or how to tailor their words and actions to fit different temperaments. The way we express ourselves is heavily influenced by our temperament, just as the way our teenagers respond is determined by theirs. When communicating with teens, we need to know how we "come across"—how our behavior is being received and interpreted by our "audience."

This chapter shouldn't be interpreted as an attempt to put people into neat little boxes or categories. The human personality is far too complex and glorious to be treated in such a mechanical fashion. Temperaments often change as a person matures. People will change their personalities to suit different home or business environments. Furthermore, temperaments can be controlled or moderated. For example, it's possible to moderate your tendency to criticize. If you tend to talk all the time, you can control this habit by making a strong commitment to listening to your teen.

As the book of Proverbs suggests, controlling one's temper, or temperament, can be better than winning a military victory. It is often extremely difficult to restrain our emotions. It may seem simpler just to lose our tempers. But it's easy to damage a relationship by voicing our feelings without thinking about how they'll be heard. Teens are especially sensitive to our expressions of feelings, and a moment's worth of venting can undo years of trust building.

Temperament analysis can help you better understand personality traits that merely frustrated or angered you in the past. This chapter will help you determine your own temperament, as well as your teen's, and discover how the interaction of different temperaments has a powerful influence over how you communicate. Understanding how these predispositions work together will give you a powerful tool for looking at and improving upon your relationship.

Discovering Your Temperament

Hippocrates (460-370 B.C.), the "father of medicine," theorized that four basic fluids found within the body of each person determined how that person acted. He claimed that on the basis of these fluids people could be classified as either Choleric, Sanguine, Phlegmatic, or Melancholy. While Hippocrates's connection between body fluids and temperament has proved unscientific, his four basic temperaments have persisted throughout the ages, and are still in use today as a convenient way to describe personality types. For our purposes, I prefer to refer to these traits by more common names that reflect their dominant characteristics: Pragmatic, Extroverted, Amiable, and Analytical.

The self-evaluation questionnaire that follows was not designed as a scientific instrument. There are no right or wrong answers. Its purpose is to help you learn about your temperament by looking at how you behave in a series of situations. For each item, write the numerical value that best represents how frequently you act in the specified way in a family setting (1 = seldom, 2 = sometimes, 3 = often, 4 = usually). (You may ask your spouse and teenager to take this inventory, or you can estimate the appropriate numbers for them.)

Section 1 Pragmatic

Husband	Wife	Teen	
			Sets very high standards for self; expects to meet them.
			Is a leader in the family; likes to take charge.
			Wants to see immediate responses to requests or instructions.
			Solves problems.
			Makes quick decisions about what should or should not be done.
			Is insensitive to feelings.
			Becomes impatient with others.
			Is viewed by others as inflexible, unyielding.
			Reacts without knowing all the facts.
			Becomes autocratic or overbearing when under tension.
			Totals

Section 2 Extroverted

Husband	Wife	Teen	
			Makes home a fun place to be.
			Is well liked by peers.
			Talks easily and often.
			Quickly sees the funny or humorous side of things.
			Lives in the present and the future, not the past.
			Is easily angered.
			Talks more than listens.
			Is perceived to use manipulation in controlling others.
			Lacks self-discipline.
			Verbally attacks others when under stress.
			Totals

Section 3 Amiable

Husband	Wife	Teen	
			Is motivated by participation in relationships.
			Looks for ways to support or encourage the family.
			Tends to agree with the family.
			Demonstrates a great deal of patience.
			Listens carefully to what the family says.
			Conforms to the family's wishes and plans.
			Tends not to confront members of the family.
			Dislikes initiating conversation.
			Passes up opportunities to share deep feelings.
			Gives in to keep the peace.
			Totals

Section 4 Analytical

Husband	Wife	Teen	
			Is motivated by the need to be right.
			Checks the accuracy of what the family says.
			Concentrates on details.
			Thinks things through before giving an answer.
			Is good at creating solutions to problems.
			Is hard to please.
			Is hesitant or indecisive when situations need an immediate response.
			Tends not to express emotion or enthusiasm in front of the family.
			Relates to the family primarily at the level of thought rather than feeling.
			Avoids confronting problems whenever possible.
			Totals

To score this inventory, add up your column in each section. The section with the highest total indicates your temperament. The short profiles that follow explain a little more about the characteristics of each of these four temperaments:

Section 1. *Pragmatic*: Emphasis on getting things done. If you scored highest in section one, you are likely to set high standards for yourself and others, want to see immediate responses to requests or instructions, like to solve problems, may cause problems by being insensitive to other's feelings by being impatient and reacting without knowing all the facts.

Section 2. *Extrovert*: Emphasis on influencing others. If you scored highest in section two, you talk easily and often, tend to see the funny or humorous side of things, and live fully in the present. You may like to control others but lack self-discipline.

Section 3. *Amiable*: Emphasis on achieving cooperation. Scoring highest in section three suggests that you are motivated by relationships, look for ways to support or encourage others, listen more than talk, and conform to other's expectations in order to maintain peace.

Section 4. *Analytical*: Emphasis on order. If you scored highest in section four, you are likely to be motivated by the need to be right, to concentrate on details, to think things through before giving an opinion, and to relate to others primarily at the level of thought rather than feeling.

You should also total and identify the temperament of each person—including your spouse and your teen—who took the test (or for whom you entered values).

As we look at how temperaments influence the way we relate to our teens, it's important to keep three points in mind. First, although each one of us has a dominant temperament, few people exhibit the traits of only one temperament. Most people demonstrate a blend of two and maybe three temperaments. Second, most people tend to change the way they express themselves depending on the context. Certain traits will dominate in the work environment, others will be more apparent at home. (For example, many people demonstrate more Analytical traits in the office than at home.) Third, and most important from our point of view, each temperament has strengths and weaknesses that reveal themselves through our patterns of communication.

Temperament Communication Patterns

What's even more important than knowing our own temperament is understanding how different patterns interact. The following chart shows how the four basic temperaments interact with each other, the misunderstandings these interactions can cause, and some useful responses. The chart can help you consider changes in your communication patterns that could lead to a better relationship with your teenager.

If you are:	And your teen is:	Your problems may include:	Responses needed:
Pragmatic	Pragmatic	Over-controlling; not allowing adequate freedom.	Restrain your tendency to over-control a situation.
	Extrovert	Too much concern for results; not enough attention to motivation.	Reduce your stress on results; increase ability to laugh.
	Amiable	Not taking enough time to listen and build a quality relationship.	Take more time to listen.
	Analytical	Too quick to make decisions; not thorough enough.	Slow down; pay more attention to detail.
Extrovert	Pragmatic	Under-concern for results; too emotional.	Acknowledge your teen's desire for results.
	Extrovert	Grandstanding; calling too much attention to yourself.	Allow your teen to be the life of the party once in a while.
	Amiable	Quickness in thinking or talking; not enough depth in relationship.	Work at listening and responding to your teen's feelings.
	Analytical	Lack of attention to detail; impulsive tendencies.	Be more careful; think about what you say before you say it.
Amiable	Pragmatic	Too much small talk; not enough decisive action.	Talk less; get to the bottom line more quickly.
	Extrovert	Apparent lack of quickness; not enough focus on the present.	Increase your quickness in responding.
	Amiable	Lack of initiative; waiting too long for your teen to initiate talk.	Take more initiative in talking; ask questions.
	Analytical	Over-concern about relationship; not enough task orientation.	Increase your interest in your teen's tasks.
Analytical	Pragmatic	Slowness to make decisions; too methodical.	Respond more quickly.
	Extrovert	Too much attention to details; not enough humor.	Relax more. Be more cheerful.
	Amiable	Not letting your teen know how you feel; insensitivity to feelings.	Strive for openness; express your feelings.
	Analytical	Arguing about who is more correct; unhealthy introspection.	Allow your teen differences of opinion.

Note how often weaknesses look like strengths pushed to an extreme. For example, the ability to make quick decisions sometimes results in poor decisions; a highly developed sense of humor may repress deep feelings. I like the idea that weaknesses may be strengths taken a bit too far. In general, it seems a lot easier to refine a strength than to overcome a weakness. It's better to try to learn to make good, quick decisions for instance, than it is to slow down the decision-making process so that we don't miss anything; it's easier to work on expressing deeper feelings through humor than it is to take a much more serious approach toward our feelings. And it means that any temperament-related communication problem can be looked at as a reason to work on improving our communication skills. As we identify patterns that cause us trouble, we can begin the process of controlling them.

Strategies for Understanding

• *Accept the differences in temperaments.* Although you and your teen may have similar temperaments, chances are good that you don't. That's okay. Our teens need to be accepted as individuals. Unless we realize that differences in temperaments are legitimate, we may fall into the trap of wanting our teens to be carbon copies of ourselves. Beware of putting teens into predetermined boxes, of categorizing them in ways that don't include the traits that make them in-dividuals. Accepting our teens' differences will make them feel more at ease, less defensive, and more un-derstanding of the character traits they don't like in us.

• *Be aware of how your temperament influences your perceptions.* School teachers and police officers complain that most parents refuse to see or believe their teen's negative behavior. Parents like to believe that it's somebody else's fault—not their teen's. Your temperament can also prevent you from seeing your teen's strengths. For example, if you are Pragmatic and your teen is Amiable, you may not fully appreciate the value of your teen's ability to establish strong friendships. If you understand your teen's temperament patterns clearly, you'll be less likely to project your own temperament onto him—and you'll have a much more realistic picture of what he's really like as a person.

• *Become more versatile by adopting the strengths of other temperaments.* You have the ability to become more versatile by developing more than one communication pattern. For example, if you tend to be animated and talkative, you can try to be more reflective and quiet. If the chart revealed temperament-related communication patterns that you think might be causing problems between you and your teen, try to widen the range of your responses to your teen. The more options you have, the more likely you'll be to come up with the right strategy for a given situation.

• *Practice open communication.* Clearing up the misunderstandings caused by the interplay of different temperaments is just one of the benefits of open communication. Open communication is honest, straightforward, and truthful and gets you straight to the heart of issues. By letting your teen know just how you feel—in a tactful and nonjudgmental way—you lessen the chance that you've been misunderstood thanks to her own temperament-related biases. Your teen wants to know how you feel and what you think. Yes, open communication does give teens a clear target for reprisals. But it is much better than avoiding or suppressing difficult issues or disagreements. A commitment to open communication can help you overcome your fear that your teen might not like what you have to say.

Temperament and Parental Teamwork

Parents need to think about how to make their unique temperaments and conversational styles work together. In most families, husbands and wives have different skills and abilities and see issues from distinctly different viewpoints. The husband may be a better talker; the wife a better listener. One may have the time-management skills of a Pragmatist; the other the discernment of an Analytical Thinker.

These differences can lead parents to compete or disagree over family issues. Or they can help parents see how much they need each other to make the family work as a team. I find that our parental teamwork is helped immeasurably when Janiece and I follow three rules:

First: *Agree on basic parenting principles.* Janiece and I often approach our parenting tasks from different viewpoints, based on our temperaments. She is a Pragmatic/Extrovert, while I am a mix between Amiable and Analytical. In order to work together as a team, we have had to think through and talk extensively about the principles we want to use in parenting our children. Here are a few that work for us.

• Don't yell. It's counter-productive.
• Build your children's self-esteem daily.
• Listen. Ask questions first; act second.
• Speak the truth, but with love.

- Allow as much freedom as possible within reasonable boundaries.
- Accept differences in temperament.
- Always be ready to forgive.
- Support each other in your roles as parents.

This last principle bears special comment. Janiece and I don't always agree on how to solve a problem with the children. If a disagreement develops in front of the children, we tell them that we need to talk the matter over, and that we will then let them know our decision. This is not dishonest; it's smart. Arguing over rules or decisions in front of the children would undermine both parents' authority. It would send the children the message that they can take sides, that they can "divide and conquer." In parenting, it's more important to be unified than it is to be "right."

Second: *Compensate for your spouse's weaknesses.* If my wife and I were both alike, one of us would be unnecessary. But I need her help and she needs mine. As a result, we've both learned to avoid criticizing the other for personal failings. Instead we try to compensate for each other, filling in the gaps where necessary, knowing that the other will be there to help us as well.

Without Janiece, I'd overlook a lot of things that the children really need to learn. Their chores would not get done. Without me, we wouldn't have as clear a handle on the differences in our children's temperaments, and the principle of "listening, then acting" would be reversed. By understanding and compensating for the weaknesses inherent in each other's temperament, we work better together as a team and do a better job of raising our children.

Third: *Draw out your spouse's strengths and help him with his weaknesses.* Each of us has strengths and talents that are still in raw form. These include character traits, attitudes, beliefs, values, and ways of communicating. You can help your spouse develop these strengths by encouraging him to make the most of his "natural resources."

On the other hand, sometimes we surprise ourselves with our pettiness, meanness, and lack of sensitivity. Most of us need help to change bad habits, and no one is in a better position to help out than our spouses. They can help us focus on the areas we need to improve in and offer positive reinforcement as we build new strengths. Happily, we can do the same for them in return.

Your spouse can be your coach, your cheerleader, your teacher. Make sure to spend as much energy on your communication and relationship with your spouse as you do with your teenager. Married couples who have a strong, healthy relationship and good communication skills are better equipped to share the load of parenting.

Taking Responsibility

Perhaps you dream of a harmonious, happy, satisfying relationship with your teen, but you sense that there is something specific about your temperament that keeps getting in the way. If so, it doesn't have to stay that way. In an inspiring and instructive book entitled *Everything I Know at the Top I Learned at the Bottom*, entrepreneur Dexter Yager writes,

> *You can change. Your personality is not set in cement. Escape the temperament trap. Don't use your knowledge of your temperament as an excuse to stay the way you are. Make yourself worthy of your dream by changing the things in your personality that need improvement.*[1]

Action Steps for Improving Your Temperament

• *Set up a chart that shows your temperament compared with that of your teen.* Write down examples for each of you from the "Your problems may include …" category in the table on page 129. See whether your teen agrees with your choices, and whether she can come up with examples of her own. Make a list or put up a sign reminding you of the conflicting traits you need to watch out for. (For example, "Warning! Perfectionist at Work!")

• *Review the section on "Understanding Temperaments" and jot down the four positive and four negative characteristics that best describe you.* Which of the negative traits are good targets for improvement? What are concrete steps you could take to change them? Decide which of these is most important to you and lay out a six-week plan for making a significant change. For example, if one of your negative characteristics is that you are insensitive to feelings, your list might look like the following:

- Ask my teen how she feels about how I talk to her.
- Ask her for suggestions on how I could show greater sensitivity.
- Make a point of trying out her suggestion once a day for six weeks—making a check mark on my desk calendar each time I make the effort.

• *Write out a set of principles based on those listed in "Temperament and Parental Teamwork" on pages 131–132. Encourage your spouse to do the same.* Share your lists and decide which could make the biggest difference in your role as parents. Take the initiative. You may find that you need to work on communication with your spouse as much as with your teenager.

CHAPTER TEN

HELPING YOUR TEENAGER MAKE IMPORTANT DECISIONS

My parents had given me everything they could possibly owe a child and more. Now it was my turn to decide and nobody ... could help me very far ...[1]

— GRAHAM GREENE

Toward the end of their high school years, teenagers begin to worry about their future. They've learned that they're facing a series of crucial decisions—choices about education, careers, relationships, and so on, that will affect their lives for years to come. It's difficult for teenagers to come to grips with these decisions—the choices can seem so new and so important.

Can you help your teen through this difficult time? More than you might think. Yes, these big decisions must be theirs, not ours. Graham Greene was right: We can't help older teens "very far." But we can show them how to ask the right questions, teach them some of the basics of making decisions, and work with them as they sort out their confusions and strike out toward their goals. Your support and encouragement for your teen during this tumultuous period can make a profound difference.

Of course, teens have a natural need to carve out their identities, to choose their own paths, to become their own persons on their own terms. Since teens resist anything that remotely resembles interference in their affairs, we need to be prepared for those moments when they're ready to listen—when they want to talk about their concerns and challenges, and are willing to accept the help we can give them.

This chapter is designed to help you prepare for the time when your daughter laments, "Mom, I don't know what I want to do with my life," or when your son states, "Dad, I'm weighing the pros and cons of going directly into the Marines or going to college." These may be cries for help; they may represent your best opportunity to help your child make good decisions about what's best for him and his future.

This chapter, therefore, takes a slightly different approach to communication. It goes beyond the mechanics we've been discussing so far—the "hows" of communication—to address the "whats"—the messages and values we want to make sure we communicate to our children.

It will help you prepare for five of the most important and most difficult decisions your teen will face: what kind of education she wants, what kind of career or vocation she wants to pursue, what role money or material things will play in her life, what she's looking for in her relationships, especially marriage, and what she believes—how she relates to religion and faith.

For each decision, I've laid out three steps that will help you to prepare. First, we'll look at the basic facts or concepts you need to keep in mind as you prepare to counsel your teenager. Next, we'll look at the key ideas or values you want to make sure to communicate to your teen. Finally, we'll practice some "door openers," strategies for starting healthy discussions with your teen.

The most important step we can take, however, is to be clear about our own values. Values give us both the starting point and the essential framework for making major decisions. They are the premises on which we base our reasoning and the standards against which we measure our options. To teach our children to make their own decisions, we need to help them establish their own values. Without values, our teens will be left adrift, rudderless, without a destination in their adult lives.

As you read about the five decisions, use the "talking points" in each section to reexamine your own values. It may have been years since you really examined the foundation for what you think and do. You can help your teen only to the extent you are willing to search out and reaffirm your inner core of values.

We also need to know *how* to talk about what we value most. As you face the issues raised in this chapter, you'll begin to apply the caring communication skills you've learned throughout this book to your teen's greatest concerns. But the techniques and strategies are just the start of the process. You'll have to muster all of the love, patience, and perseverance you can even to get a hearing.

Of course the results will be worth the effort. Seeing your child test and then accept the values you've tried to teach can be one of the most rewarding passages of parenting. It's like seeing a garden bloom out of the "value" seeds that you've planted over the years. When your child acquires a healthy, fully-grown set of values of her own, she is ready to make her own decisions and chart her own path in the adult world. For a parent, this is the equivalent of rounding the far turn and heading down the home stretch. It's finally time for the "payoff" for the hard work and the self-sacrifice you've made for your teen. Not all parent/teen relationships survive the adolescent years, and just hearing our teens say, "Thanks, Mom. That means a lot to me" or "Thanks, Dad. That's just what I needed to hear," is a real victory for parents.

As we talk about values, you may find that yours differ from those in the examples below. Or, perhaps you haven't given some of the issues much thought. It's important that you make the effort to clarify your own beliefs and to set an example for your teens of a life led according to values. The discussions here reflect fairly mainstream values, but the process can easily be adapted to incorporate your own beliefs. My hope is that you'll see any similarities in our values as reinforcement and support for your efforts, and any differences as an opportunity to identify and clarify for yourself—and for your teen—the values that are most important in life.

Education: What Do I Want to Know?

During the summer before their senior year of high school, our teens received a host of brochures in the mail advertising particular colleges or fields of study. If your teenager has reached this decision stage, you know the intensity of his concerns. You may hear him make statements that demonstrate the anxiety he feels:

"This is a big deal." "I really am growing up." "I'm going to have to decide what I want to do with my life." "What kind of training do I want? Where can I get it?" "Do I really want to go to college?" "Will I be accepted?" "Can I afford it?" "What happens if I fail?" "Help!"

Key Perspectives on Education

Here are a few key ideas that will help you prepare to respond when your teen needs your help.

• Is my teen ready for college? Children learn and mature at different rates. Our school systems group children according to chronological age as matter of convenience; graduating from high school doesn't necessarily mean that they're mentally and emotionally ready for college.

• Should my teen go to college? Not every child should, even if mentally capable of succeeding at that level of education. A trade or technical school or a first job may be more in line with your teen's needs and aspirations. If you try to persuade your teen to go to college when she's not sure it's right for her, you may cause her to feel guilty or inadequate, bringing on long-term unhappiness.

• Which colleges are best? Not all college educations are the same. Vast differences exist among colleges regarding their academic standards and their educational theories. Do we know what their standards are—and do we agree with them? Does a college place a higher priority on "life adjustment skills" or on "intellectual content and discipline"? Is there a balance?

• What do I have to offer? Am I encouraging the development of my teen's talents and interests? Am I encouraging the study and reading habits they'll need for higher education? If college is not an option, have I helped my teen explore other possibilities for getting the knowledge and skills they need, such as correspondence schools, continuing education seminars, and night or weekend classes?

• What are my resources? How will my teen's education be funded? Does my teen know about scholarship aid? If not, where can my teen get the information? (See the Resources section in the back of this book.)

Key Points to Make about Education

Consider passing on the following values about education to your teen. Hopefully, this list will stimulate you to think of additional values.

• Learning can be enjoyable. Letting our minds grapple with difficult concepts and discovering big ideas doesn't need to be drudgery. If we learn how to think and approach the process with a positive attitude, learning really can be fun.

• Gaining wisdom should be a major life goal. It's not just a matter of learning during school. Neither is it just preparing for a specific job or career. Wisdom equips us for life, and we ought to pursue it with gusto and determination in all our reading, observation, and experience.

• Education never ends. It's a lifelong process of training the mind, gaining knowledge, seeking the truth. An open mind and a teachable spirit are essential. At the same time, we can know some things with certainty without knowing everything. A college freshman doesn't know as much as his professor of philosophy, but he just might have a clearer glimpse of the truth.

• "Dig deep, irrigate widely." I am indebted to my friend, Dr. Ken Pike, former head of the Linguistics Department at the University of Michigan, for this bit of wisdom. The image conveys a value I want to transfer to my children: thinking well may be difficult work, but the deeper we go the broader and more useful the application.

• Reason and faith are complementary. The scientific process is built on the faith that certain natural laws will continue to hold true, whether or not they are fully understood. Water always boils at 212 degrees at sea level. Gravity always pulls objects heavier than air to the ground. Without faith in natural laws, reason would be useless. The technology that took us to the moon was based on faith in the natural laws of the universe. King Solomon expressed the complementary relationship of faith and reason when he said, "The fear of the Lord is the beginning of wisdom" (Proverbs 1:7).

• Searching for wisdom can lead to spiritual insight. As King Solomon wrote to his own son,

> My son, if you accept my words ... turning your ear to wisdom and applying your heart to understanding, and if you call out for insight and cry aloud for understanding, and if you look for it as for silver and search for it as for hidden treasure, then you will understand the fear of the Lord and find the knowledge of God (Proverbs 2:1-4).

Conversation Starters

How do we communicate our values effectively? Granted, a lot of values are "caught instead of taught," but we can also try conversation starters that make use of our teens' "moments of readiness" to transfer our values.

• Read good books. If something interests you, talk about it. It may encourage your teen to read, and it may spark her interest in big ideas.

• Share your insights. Maybe something you heard or read strikes you as fascinating or as the answer to a puzzling question. Perhaps it gives you a new perspective on an issue. Talk about it briefly and with enthusiasm.

• Talk to your teens about news events and invite their opinions on topics that may be controversial. Let your children know what you think and why you think that way, but let them know that you're genuinely open to their ideas. If you do, your conversation can be a mutually satisfying discussion instead of an argument.

• Invite your teen's questions and comments. Never ridicule an idea that comes from one of your children. Create an atmosphere in the home where it is safe to express even half-formed ideas, where each thought is treated with respect.

• Admit your mistakes of logic or reason. "I guess that doesn't make a whole lot of sense, does it?" "Well, that proves I was wrong." Demonstrating your honesty and humility will increase your credibility.

• Reward discovery. Comment on the new insights or logical connections that your teen makes. Praise him publicly by saying:

"That's a neat idea.

"I think that's a profound point."

"That sounds interesting. Tell me more."

• Listen actively. Ask questions. Look your teen in the eye and show interest in what she is saying. Encourage the development of her thinking process through your comments:

"Have you thought about what you would do if ...?"

"I see. How did you arrive at that conclusion?"

"Then what?"

"I'm not sure I see the connection."

Vocation: What Will I Do With My Life?

In one of our "heart-to-heart" talks, Jud said,

"Dad, I don't know what kind of work I should go into. I think about it and try to weigh all the factors, but nothing comes clear. Sometimes I want to know so badly that it hurts, like a pain right here in my chest."

Our teens probably think a lot more about their future than we realize. They'll have to experience much of the thinking—and the hurting—themselves. Yet at some point we went through the same process. Perhaps we are still wondering whether we made the right decision, or maybe we're in the process of changing to a new line of work and understand the pressures. Examining our own experience can help us help when our teens ask us, "What will I do with my life? How do I decide? What factors should I consider?"

Key Perspectives on Careers

• Management experts estimate that nearly 80 percent of all Americans are dissatisfied with their work and career. Surveys have shown that work is often associated with apathy, boredom, nervousness, shouting matches, and daily humiliations.... Job dissatisfaction can lead to boredom, lack of purpose in life, and even a sense of hopelessness. Is it because people chose their careers without giving them adequate thought, without a sense of mission, and without clear values as a basis for their decision?

• A study by the National Assessment of Educational Progress has concluded that most students in high school today do not have realistic expectations about their careers. Only 35 percent of seventeen-year-olds said that they had spoken with the school advisor about their career aspirations and plans.

Sources of information such as the *Occupational Outlook Handbook* (from the Department of Labor), the *Encyclopedia of Careers* (Doubleday), and the *Dictionary of Occupational Titles* (Department of Labor), are readily available and can help bridge this information gap.

• Most jobs require strong people skills. For both professionals and inexperienced workers, few problems at work have to do with technical skills, training, knowledge, information, or intelligence. Most (85 percent, according to one study) are caused by the inability to communicate well.

• Extensive surveys conducted by the Institute for Social Research at the University of Michigan suggest that long hours of part-time work by high school students are linked with weak school performance, low college aspirations, and higher drug use.[2]

Key Points to Make about Careers

• Work can be a positive means of expressing our talents and interests. Contrary to what some people think, work is not a "curse." It's possible to find both immense enjoyment and fulfillment in work.

• The value of work is not determined by the amount of money we make. It's a sad commentary on our society's priorities that football players get million-dollar contracts while our children's teachers survive on subsistence wages. A mother's investment in the lives of her children is, at the very minimum, as valuable as the work of an athlete or business executive.

• A sense of mission in our work can prevent it from becoming a meaningless routine. The word *vocation* comes from the Latin word *vocare*, which means "to call." It refers to the idea that one's work is a "calling" from God. If our teens understand that a prospective career can be their calling, their work will take on meaning far beyond that produced by money or prestige.

• One's vocation ought to be characterized by a passion for excellence. Our parents taught us, "If it's worth doing, it's worth doing well." Excellence results from diligence, our constant and careful attempt to do our best. Put your whole self into your work and aim for the highest standard of which you are capable.

• Overwork is counterproductive. Perfectionists and "workaholics" have been overwhelmed and mastered by their work. Overwork almost always causes stress, fatigue, impatience, and the neglect of important relationships and responsibilities. Not surprisingly, the quality of the work also declines. During the French Revolution, the government decided to do away with "Sabbath Observance" and institute a seven-day work schedule designed to create greater productivity. The experiment failed as the health and motivation of the workers deteriorated.

Conversation Starters
• Ask questions that will help your teen think about possible careers.

"What kinds of activities do you feel you are good at?" (Mental, manual, interpersonal?)

"What kind of people would you enjoy working with?" (Thinkers, practitioners, craftsmen, decision makers, leaders, followers, a combination?)

"What area of the country would you want to settle in?" (Near or far away from home? What kind of climate and terrain? Urban or rural?)

"What kind of hours would you like to work?" (Flexible, strictly nine-to-five, nights, days?)

"What would your goals be in your work? What would you want to accomplish? What would make you feel good about yourself?"

• Avoid interrogating your teen! These questions require some thought and some sensitivity on your part. Make sure that you ask them at the right time, in the right place, and with the right attitude. If you want to be of help, it's essential that your teen knows you accept and welcome her ideas, even if you don't agree with them.

• Be careful not to kill your teen's enthusiasm for an idea by overreacting—even if the idea seems senseless or impossible to you. Avoid making judgmental statements like "There aren't many jobs in that field" or "I doubt if you could stand the pressure." Keep in mind that the creative process is full of dead ends, false starts, and half-formed answers—and that designing his future is one of the most creative things your teen will ever have to do. Trust the process—gathering information, brainstorming about possibilities, examining alternatives, gaining wisdom through experience, and open-ended communication—to carry him past wrong paths.

• Encourage your teen to take the Strong Vocational Interest Test or some other standard test (perhaps through her school's guidance office) that will help her see how her interests compare with those who are successful in the career fields she's considering.

• Help your teen learn more about what different careers are really like. Our family decided to ask friends who work in a variety of careers to come for dinner. Questions like the following provoked stimulating discussion:

"What is the nature of your work? What do you actually do from day to day?"

"Why did you choose your line of work?"

"What were some of the steps that led you to your choice of work?"

"If you could make your decision over again, what would you do differently?"

"What are some of the problems you encounter in your work? How do you handle them?"

"What do you like about your work? What keeps you in it?"

Yes, it required extra effort to plan such encounters, and sometimes our kids weren't so sure it was a good idea, but the resulting discussions were usually fascinating and helpful.

• Talk openly about your own work, your disappointments and sources of satisfaction. If possible, invite your teen to spend a day at work with you and to work alongside you. Treat your teen as you would an esteemed friend or highly valued new employee. Approach the venture with the attitude that your teen is joining the "team" for the day. Think about what your teen might do that would help him or her understand your work.

• Make sure your teen knows that his career is his decision and responsibility, not yours. If you try to control the process, he will resist, but he will always appreciate your efforts to help him make his own decision.

• Make sure your teen doesn't feel pressured to choose the same career you did. Beware of the subtle pressures your teen might feel if several generations in your family have chosen a particular line of work. You may have to work hard to convince your teen that she really is free to choose. If a career choice based on family history turned out to be a bad fit, you would be at least partly responsible for the problems. Besides, such pressures demonstrate a lack of respect for your teen's individuality and unique potential.

• If necessary, help your teen with the details of job hunting. For many teens the process of looking for a job involves too many "unknowns," and can seem like an impassable barrier. Help your teen get started by sharing a few of the simpler tasks—show him how to fill out a form and make a phone call for information, for example, or suggest how and where to do research,—but don't do the work for him. One mother not only called prospective employers for her daughter, she also answered all of the employer's questions. She wanted to help too much. She ended up giving her daughter the impression she wasn't capable of handling the situation herself. Another mother told her daughter, "I'll stay as close or as far away as you wish. You take the lead. I know you can do it."

• Show your teen how to check the bookstore and library for resources. Make sure he consults with the school guidance counselor and others who may be of help. Taking the time to get the right kind of help at the start can help your teen avoid days and weeks of aimless exploring.

Money: What Are My Priorities?

Chuck Colson tells a story about a man at a car rental counter who insisted that he needed a black Continental because everyone going to his New Year's Eve party would be driving black Continentals. On the man's tee shirt was this inscription: "The one who dies with the most toys, wins." Did the man really believe that motto? Is it an adequate philosophy for life? Did anyone help him when he was a young man to sort what his priorities would be?

Key Perspectives on Money

• Americans earn more per person than any people in the history of the world, yet the overwhelming majority of those who reach 65 have saved little or no money. Out of every hundred, only two are financially independent, twenty-three are forced to continue working just to survive, and seventy-five are dependent on social security, friends, relatives, or charity.[3]

• A growing number of college freshmen are concerned with little besides making a living. According to a twenty-year study by the Cooperative Institutional Research Program (CIRP), accumulating money seems to be especially important. While twenty years ago more than 80 percent of freshmen chose "developing a meaningful philosophy of life" as an essential goal, today only 41 percent consider it a worthy goal. CIRP pollsters Alexander Austin and Kenneth Green observe: "It may be that some students view making a lot of money as a kind of 'philosophy of life' itself."[4]

• People who misunderstand or aren't clear about their priorities can work a lifetime trying to accumulate money, trying to buy peace of mind and happiness without ever achieving either.

• The media's emphasis (especially in advertising) on "having it all" is partly responsible for the increased materialism of our society. To avoid being taken prisoner by materialism (thinking that we're somehow inadequate or underprivileged if we don't own all of the latest *things*), we need to talk openly with our teens about what materialism is and how and why we should try to rise above it.

• If teenagers work a steady job or are freely given money by their parents, they often experience "premature affluence." Since they don't have the major financial responsibilities (car payments, mortgages, college loans, and so on) that eat up most of an adult's paycheck, they have plenty of disposable income, and as a result may develop spending habits that are tough to break. The result? They end up financially trapped and feel like failures when their finances come back down to earth.

• Money management is best learned in the home at an early age. Keep in mind that your teen is more likely to follow your example than what you say.

Key Points to Make about Money

• Money is a tool that can be used for good or evil. It is not money that is the root of all evil but the "love of money" (I Timothy 6:10). Someone has said, "If we make money our god, it will plague us like the devil."

• Wise stewardship of our resources involves learning the skills of planning, budgeting, saving, investing, and time management. If we consciously distinguish between needs and wants, and budget to meet our needs first, we will avoid financial bondage.

• Giving to help meet the physical and spiritual needs of others can be a source of happiness.

• Try to live—and teach your teen to live—by a priority system that puts money and material goods in their place. Facing an early death from brain cancer, "bad boy" Lee Atwater, former President Bush's 1988 campaign manager, found his perspective had changed:

> I acquired more wealth, power, and prestige than most. But you can acquire all you want and still feel empty. What power wouldn't I trade for a little more time with my family? What price wouldn't I pay for an evening with friends? It took a deadly illness to put me eye to eye with that truth, but it is a truth that the country, caught up in its ruthless ambitions and moral decay, can learn on my dime.[5]

• The secret to real, lasting success in business is compassion. Rich DeVos, one of the wealthiest of men in America, makes a strong case for this rather surprising fact in his book *Compassionate Capitalism*.

> Regrettably, there have always been (and will always be) greedy, uncaring capitalists who think it's all right to make a profit even if that process leads to the suffering of people and to the destruction of our planet. Compassionate capitalists still want to make a profit, but they are determined

that real profits come when the good of people and the planet comes first.[6]

• You can't put a price on contentment. Everyone wants peace of mind, but it's not for sale. It does not result from the accumulation of things but from building human relationships, achieving personal goals, and pursuing things that really matter.

Conversation Starters

• Talk with your teen about your own financial decisions, including what you have learned from your mistakes as well as your successes.

• Make sure that your teen understands the basics of budgeting. Most teens focus on their immediate needs and wants. It's hard for them to understand why they need to save money, or the long-range consequences of "buy now, pay later." Let her take a look at your family budget, or work through with her how much money, and how many hours of work, it takes to pay for a meal, a car, a house, or four years in college.

• Ask your teen to keep a weekly budget sheet for two weeks and to record all income and expenses. Help her see the importance of knowing where the money goes.

• Discuss your values regarding money and possessions with your teen. Talk about the differences between wants and needs. Ask her to make a list of things she would like to have—and then put each into one of the two categories.

Marriage: Whom Will I Marry?

It may sound clinical, but psychiatrist Harry Stack Sullivan described love well when he said, "When the satisfaction or security of another person becomes as significant to one as is one's own satisfaction and security, then the state of love exists."[7]

Still, most teens have questions. "If I feel love for more than one person, how will I know which is the right one for me? Is something wrong with me if I don't have strong feelings for anyone right now? What if a friend feels strongly about me, but I don't feel as strongly about that friend? Whom will I marry? How will I know when I'm ready?"

These are not easy questions to answer. Many smaller decisions must be made before the big one—about whom your teen will spend the rest of his life with—can be answered. Ordinarily, our teens don't ask these questions until they've developed a great deal of independence from our influence, but the issues are so big and so important that we can still expect our teens to look to us for some guidance.

Key Perspectives on Marriage

• In 1870, one out of every thirty-four marriages ended in divorce; two generations ago, the numbers had risen to one in every twelve marriages; in the last generation, they'd risen to one in every three. At present, almost one out of every two marriages is dissolved.

• In psychological terms, "like attracts like." One key ingredient in happy marriages is compatibility—similarity in areas such as faith, education, family background, interests, and attitudes. In *Finding the Love of Your Life*, Neil Clark Warren states, "Research findings are highly consistent: The most stable marriages are those involving two people with many similarities.[8]

• One study surveyed couples who had been happily married for thirty years or more. The common ingredient? Good communication—the ability to listen well and express thoughts and feelings without fear of reprisal.

• Considerable evidence suggests that problems in marriages can be anticipated—through careful observation—as early as the dating period. We can help our teens by giving them standards they can use to evaluate the behavior, character, and values of the people they're involved with.

• In a study of three thousand families, researchers Nick Stinnett and John Defrain found six major characteristics of strong families. Members of healthy families:

1. Are committed to the family
2. Spend time together
3. Are good communicators
4. Express their appreciation for each other
5. Have a spiritual commitment
6. Are able to solve problems in a crisis

• Marital intimacy is the result of hard work—an effort of the heart, mind, soul, and will. Even when couples seem compatible, it's still not easy to predict why certain marriages last and some don't. Many strong marriages, however, demonstrate the following:

- A shared faith that the couple practices together
- A deepening and developing love between the two that each communicates daily in ways the partner understands and appreciates
- Mutual trust and respect
- Physical attraction
- Intellectual compatibility
- Similar work interests
- A belief in marriage as a lifelong commitment
- The ability to talk honestly about thoughts and feelings
- The ability to listen deeply
- Mutual respect and admiration for each other's character
- The support and acceptance of both families
- A willingness to compromise to promote the other's happiness
- Similar goals and plans for family, vocation, lifestyle
- Similar financial priorities
- The ability to resolve conflicts
- A willingness and readiness to forgive
- A shared sense of humor

- In a chapter entitled, "You and the Person You May Marry," psychologist Irene Kassorla lists some of the danger signs that may signal a poor choice.

- Pressure applied by the other
- Dissatisfaction with the other's expressions of affection
- Strong parental disapproval
- Constant quarreling and bickering
- Recurrent doubts
- The desire to make changes in the partner's personality
- Disapproval of partner's friends
- A relationship that "clicks" in only one area
- A wish to alter the ambitions, dreams, or goals of the partner
- Feelings of regret regarding the engagement
- Repeated episodes of "breaking the engagement"
- Either partner's excessively close attachment to parents
- Considering the demands of the partner unfair or irrational[9]

• "Falling" in and out of love is a normal adolescent activity. Dating gives your teen valuable experience in interacting with different personalities and learning what really matters in a relationship.

• Many teens are confused about the difference between love and infatuation. In response to the plea of one young woman, Ann Landers distinguished the two this way:

> Infatuation leaps into bloom. Love usually takes root and grows one day at a time. Infatuation is accompanied by a sense of uncertainty. You are stimulated and thrilled, but not really happy. You are miserable when he is absent. You can't wait until you see him again.

> Love begins with a feeling of security. You are warm with a sense of his nearness, even when he is away. Miles do not separate you. You want him near, but near or far, you know he's yours and you can wait.

> Infatuation says, "We must get married right away. I can't risk losing him." Love says, "Don't rush into anything. You are sure of one another. You can plan your future with confidence.[10]

Key Points to Make about Marriage

• Teach the values of chastity before marriage, faithfulness after marriage.[11] The primary reason for living by these values is not simply that it's smart, safe, or psychologically healthy, but that the results of ignoring them damage relationships and hurt other people.

• Emphasize the importance of lifelong commitment. Since emotions are unpredictable, any marriage based on emotion or erotic feeling alone is likely to fail. "As long as we both shall love" never has the strength or staying power as the commitment "as long as we both shall live."

• A "pair bonding" takes place when a man and a woman choose to leave their parents and create a new identity together, a new union. As parents, we need to communicate to our children that we view their marriage as a major transition—a shift from parental allegiance to a new allegiance to their spouse—and that we will not hold them back by clinging to them.

• Evaluating a relationship requires that each partner get to know the other's innermost thoughts, feelings, preferences, instincts, biases, and dreams. It takes time for couples to get to know each other well enough to evaluate their readiness for the complexity and demands of marriage. They need time to build a strong foundation of deep understanding, trust, and mutual goals.

• A commitment to practicing good communication is one of the best ways to prevent problems from occurring in a marriage. Closeness through communication can help couples bridge differences, deal with new problems, and promote the experience of sharing that most married couples find so rewarding. See the Resources section at the back of the book for further help on achieving closeness through good communication.

Conversation Starters

• If your teen seems interested, share the details of your own search for "the right one" to marry. Include the humor, mistakes, feelings, hopes, and dreams, but don't get carried away and talk forever. Show your enthusiasm for the subject. Let your teen ask for more.

• Talk about the difficulties that you've faced in your own marriage, and how you've tried to overcome these barriers. Some teens have unrealistic expectations about marriage. They need to know that there are likely to be difficulties, conflicts, and misunderstandings—but that with a strong commitment, it is possible to work your way past them.

• Encourage your teen to think about what characteristics he would value most in a potential mate. On a scale of one (low value) to ten (high value), ask your teen to rank the indicators of compatibility discussed above. Keep in mind that this is just an exercise and that rankings are likely to change over time. Be careful not to judge his answers—your job at this point is to listen carefully and ask questions that will help him work out his own notions of what can provide genuine happiness.

• Talk to your teen about your values. After thinking through what you believe is important for a happy marriage, try to draw your teen into a dialogue by encouraging questions and listening intently.

• When your teen wants to talk about relationships or marriage, listen. Ask questions gently, and make statements in a non-threatening way so that your teen keeps talking, discovering, learning. You can make supportive, encouraging statements along the lines of:

"This relationship seems really important to you."

"I sense that you are troubled by the way Ken talks to you."

"I've never seen you so excited about anyone as you are about Kimberly. She seems very special."

"You've talked about a number of characteristics you are looking for in a marriage partner. Which do you think are most important to a healthy marriage?"

• Give your teen books that help her ask herself good questions. Good books or other resources can sometimes help teenagers deal with anxieties that they're afraid or embarrassed to share with their parents. See the Resources section for suggestions.

• If it seems appropriate, pray for your children's future marriage in their hearing. Some teens never hear their parents pray for them. They miss a great source of support, encouragement, and guidance. Pray for your teen and for the person your teenager will one day marry.

Faith: What Will I Believe?

In *The Closing of the American Mind*, Allan Bloom notes that at one time the family was the center of religious training.

My grandparents were ignorant people by today's standards. But their home was spiritually rich because all things done in it found their origin in the Bible's commandments. Their simple faith and practices linked them to the great thinkers who have dealt with the same material.[12]

According to Bloom, if students today come to the university with no sense of "the great revelations, epics and philosophies," part of the reason is "the dreariness of the family's spiritual landscape ..."[13]

Teens ask: Why be moral? Why should I act any differently from my classmates? Why shouldn't I do whatever I feel at the moment? Although we can give several answers to these questions, one of the best is our belief in a personal God who has given us direction on how to live. Teens need to question and make decisions about their faith. As in all important issues, their parent's example is often their strongest influence.

Key Perspectives on Faith

• Young people who say faith is important are more likely to demonstrate moral behavior and participate in service activities; they also exhibit fewer self-destructive practices than other teens. On the basis of their study, Merton and Irene Strommen report that adolescents with a genuine faith are less racially prejudiced and less likely to be involved in such antisocial activities as fighting, vandalism, shoplifting, cheating at school, or lying to parents.[14]

• According to the Strommens, a democratic-authoritative parenting style that includes trust, spending time together as a family, and the open expression of love is closely linked to whether children develop a liberating, challenging, outgoing faith.[15]

• The adolescent years are characterized by increasing doubt. Teenagers doubt both themselves and the authority figures in their life. Yet, since adolescence is also a time of discovery, we can anticipate that our teens will show new interest in attempting to understand the mysteries of faith and religion. Teenagers need an environment in which they can ask questions and express their doubts—that encourages rather than stifles their spiritual questioning. Parents can play an essential role in seeing that their teens feel comfortable exploring the concepts and practical aspects of faith.

• Parents can try to encourage their teen's faith through discussion, but the most important factor is parental example. If the parents' faith is characterized by genuine devotion, honesty, repentance, and grateful obedience, the teenager's faith is likely to reflect the same qualities.

• Some teens will rebel regardless of the quality of their parents' faith, but I believe that where this faith is strong, the rebellion may be temporary. Teenagers want to understand their parents' spiritual journey. They will be drawn to faith if it is an everyday part of their family life, and not merely a routine.

Key Points to Make about Faith

Here are some basic questions about faith that parents need to ask and answer for themselves before they can help their teens develop a strong, rewarding faith.

• "What do I believe? What do I practice? What do I want my children to believe? How can I best communicate my values to them? What are they learning about faith from my example?"

• "Can teens know for sure that they will be with God after they die? If so, on what basis?"

- "What is the nature of human beings? Are we basically good at heart or sinful by nature?"
- "Who or what is God? Is God personal? Is God a God of love or justice or both?"
- "How can a person be right with God?"
- "What does it mean to believe or have faith?"

Conversation Starters

- Create an atmosphere of openness about your faith. Let your children know that your faith in God is real by expressing your own questions and insights, your struggles and your gratitude. For example:

"As I was jogging last night, I began to think about you children and how important you are to me. You really are a blessing to us—a source of joy. I want you to know that I thank God for you every day."

- Allow the adventure of your faith to shine through in your daily life. I will always remember the many ways my parents taught me the immediacy of faith. For example, when I was six I desperately wanted a bike, but since we had a large family, we did not have enough money to buy one. In her book, *Consecrated Hands*, my mother tells the story:

> One morning at the breakfast table after we had just finished our family prayers, and each of the children had prayed that in some way Paul would be able to have a bike, there was a knock at the door. It was our next-door neighbor, who said, "Bill wants to sell his bike, but before he puts an ad in the paper he wondered if Paul might be interested in having it. He will charge Paul only $5.00." I wish you could have seen the eyes of our children. Why, God had answered their prayers that very morning![16]

God doesn't always answer prayers like that. Good thing. The next morning I started praying for a horse! However, the point my parents impressed upon me from childhood was that our faith must be a part of our daily life. It was then natural for me as a teenager to sense that I could draw strength and courage from my belief in God in the midst of some very difficult and confusing times.

- Let your faith play an important role in your decision making. When a church in Tennessee called me to be an associate minister, I said no twice. I had been the pastor of a church in Florida for eleven years. We loved the people and felt there was still much work to be done. However, when we received the third call from the church in Tennessee, we talked about it as a family. Jud and Jessica pointed out that they would have to leave lifetime friends. Eight-year-old Jessica said, "Dad, we have no relatives in Memphis and if we go there I will never have any friends again." For several days we talked and prayed about it as a family. Then at the dinner table one night I said that it was time to make a decision. I asked each member of the family the same question, beginning with Jessica. "On the basis of what you know about this decision, Jessica, do you think that it is God's will that we go to Memphis?" Through her tears, she said "Yes!" The family's sense of God's will was unanimous. When we arrived in Memphis, we found that there were five friends Jessica's age on our street. Having prayed for direction, she knew whom to thank.

• Read the Bible together as a family. My parents read us Bible stories with enthusiasm and expression, as if they were the greatest stories ever told. We listened with rapt attention to the high drama of David and Goliath, Daniel in the Lions' Den, and the conversion of the Apostle Paul. As we grew older, we sensed the depth of feeling in the Psalms, in Solomon's search for an adequate philosophy of life, and the amazing grace of God. At the very least this practice gives you an opportunity to spend valuable time with your children. At best, it can be a powerful way to teach your children the value of faith in their lives.

Action Steps for Helping Teens Make Major Life Decisions

• *Write the five decision areas* (Education, Vocation, Money, Marriage, and Faith) *on a small sheet of paper.* After each heading, write a one-sentence description of how you think your teen feels about the decision, and add your estimate of how often he thinks about it. Check out the accuracy of your assumptions in an informal discussion with your teen.

• *Select the decision areas you feel are most important to your teen at this time.* Write down a few "conversation starters" that you feel might help you start a conversation on the subject with your teen. (Try adapting some of the suggestions above to your specific situation.) Initiate a conversation with your teen on the subject as soon as possible. Pay careful attention to how you're delivering your message—it's important to be relaxed and sensitive to your teen's interest level.

• *After reading through all five sections, decide where you most need to reassess or rethink your own values.* Make a list of what your concerns are, and set aside a specific time to think about the subject. It might help to set your thoughts down in a letter to yourself.

• *If your teen needs additional help or information in one of the five areas, decide what steps you will take to motivate your teen to get the help he or she needs.*

My plan is to:

_____

_____

_____.

CHAPTER ELEVEN

RESPONDING TO MAJOR PROBLEMS

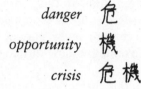

danger

opportunity

crisis

Just as the word for crisis in Chinese combines the characters for danger and opportunity, the difficult transition that teens make during adolescence offers both invaluable opportunities and real dangers. Guiding a teenager through the crises of adolescence can give you openings to talk to them about your most significant values, your philosophy of life, your views on self-discipline, the relation of sex and marriage, your responsibility for raising healthy-minded children, and the purpose and meaning of life.

Unfortunately, the dangers that our teenagers face are also real. Psychologist David Elkind writes, "The epidemic of teenage problem behavior in America today is serious and frightening."[1] As they go through the process of forming their own identity, teenagers are often highly vulnerable to outside influences. And in our culture, their parents and teachers are not the only influences on their development. In many cases, their attitudes and beliefs are also being shaped by powerful elements in our culture that have little or no interest in helping them grow up to be healthy, independent adults.

In this chapter, we'll look at five common problem areas and what you can do to help your teenager cope with the dangers of each.

You may very well be able to avoid most of these problems. After all, one of the primary benefits of working on your communication skills and building the stronger bonds I've stressed throughout this book is to prevent them from happening to you.

Still, like it or not, almost every parent of a teenager faces real, sometimes dangerous situations as teen experiments, tests limits, and establishes his or her independence. Most parents don't understand the scope or scale of these problems or how to confront them—until they're confronted with them during a crisis. The self-control and listening skills you've learned about in earlier chapters will be invaluable when you face more serious problems, and the ideas and suggestions in this chapter can help you prepare to deal with them successfully. I recommend that you read this material even if you've been lucky enough to avoid these issues so far. As a parent, you know how difficult it is to predict when problems will arise.

Some of the material in this chapter may be difficult for you to face. Most parents don't want to admit that their teen has serious problems that will require them to take action. But if our overall goal is to help our teenagers overcome the dangers they face and make the most of their opportunities, it's important to take a hard objective look at just what the problems are. Let's dig in.

Fighting for Our Children's Hearts and Minds

In today's media-saturated world, skilled professional communicators present our teens with powerful and influential images of sexuality, drugs, and violence. Their portrayal of these volatile and controversial issues is based on what they think will attract an audience, rather than on what's best for our teens. Part of our challenge as parents is to act as a counter-balance to the lessons and values our teens absorb from the media.

One of the most powerful influences affecting our teens, for example, is popular, or rock, music. Although rock music can be a force for good, the message of some groups is clearly anti-social and anti-life. Their music and promotional videos have been turned into a new, powerful form of violent entertainment. Beamed into 23.5 million households through rock videos and MTV, the pervading message of some of the music is that life is cheap and sexual violence is fun.

David Elkind writes:

Clearly the most underestimated influence on young people today is the record business. Perhaps because most adults find the level of sound obnoxious, the harmonics jarring, and the lyrics incomprehensible, we prefer to ignore the impact of rock music on our offspring.[2]

Ignore it? We can't. The stakes are too high. We can't ignore the images, the words, the philosophies that can destroy the souls and sometimes the bodies of our youth.

In an article entitled, "How Shock Rock Harms Our Kids," Peggy Mann reports that several sixth-graders asked their music teacher about the meaning of some rock-music lyrics. The message of one album was spelled out on the album cover, "We're possessed by all that's evil; the death of your God we demand. We spit at the virgin you worship, and sit at Lord Satan's left hand."[3]

The next day a host of parents called the school, incensed that the teacher would mention Satanism to their children. However, as the author states,

> *These irate parents had probably never listened to the records their kids were buying. Like many other adults, they didn't realize that some of today's rock music extols everything from rape, incest, and homosexuality to sadomasochism and bestiality—in words too graphic to be printed here.*[4]

Some parents are vaguely aware of the lyrics on their teens' CDs and on MTV, but they tend to assume their kids don't really listen to the words since they can't understand the words themselves. This is not necessarily true.

According to *Rolling Stone* magazine, 48 percent of the sixties generation—the generation that gave rock music its biggest push, many of whom are now parents themselves—see today's rock music as a "bad influence" on young people. They support a rating system for records similar to the one in place for movies. Says rock star Bruce Springsteen, "In many ways what's happening in music today is very corrupting. Let's help our children toss out the garbage."[5]

And rock music is just one part of the problem. Almost every medium presents what can only be called sociopathological behavior as exciting, desirable, normal. Mainstream movies offer splatter and gore as entertainment, daytime television shows infidelity, dishonesty, and unhealthy relationships as part and parcel of an interesting lifestyle, and books and comics casually portray drug use and violence as proper subjects for amusement.

This is why it's so essential that we develop our caring communication skills. If we want to have nearly as much influence over our teens as the media does, we must learn to be nearly as effective as communicators. We can't afford to be intimidated by the size or scope of this challenge! We are fighting for the minds of our teens. We must win for their sake!

What You Can Do:

• *Set a good example.* One expert on teens and the media says that adolescents often ask, "What about the novels my mom reads or my dad's movies? My parents' media are just as bad!"[6] To be persuasive, we have to "walk our talk," demonstrating our sincerity through the way we act. We can model respect for women as well as men, for young and old as well as middle-aged, for every human being regardless of color, race, or creed. With this kind of example to learn from, our teens stand a good chance of developing self-respect, as well.

• *Establish media standards for your family.* Standards are restrictions imposed for positive reasons. Should we allow movies or music that promote hatred, express rage, extol sexual violence, or glorify suicide, the occult, and drugs into our homes? Of course not. But why not? Because teens need to learn just how precious life is. To treat anything that degrades life as entertainment cheapens the value of life—and sends a powerful message to your child about his own worth.

• *Get to know more about your teen's favorite videos, movies, books, music, and TV programs.* Find out who her favorite singers, actors, and groups are. Watch the movies, listen to the lyrics, flip through the comics. To be credible with our teens, we have to know what we're talking about.

Susan Baker of the Parents Music Resource Center advises parents, "Instead of shouting, 'Cut down that noise!' listen to the lyrics and talk about them in light of your family's values. As a parent, you have every right to decide what kind of messages you want in your house."[7]

• *Talk to your teen about the philosophies of life represented by their favorite TV shows, videos, movies, and rock groups.* Ask your teen what these themes mean. If you feel the themes are harmful, tell your teen openly, firmly, and without getting angry or taking a judgmental attitude. Use your best listening and talking skills to teach them how to be more sensitive to these messages. For more information, you can also order the rock video "Rising to the Challenge," published by the Parents Music Resource Center, 1500 Arlington Boulevard, Arlington, VA 22209.

• *Calculate the ratio between the amount of time your teen spends under the influence of the popular media and the amount of time she spends talking to you.* Keep an informal timesheet for at least a week. Are you satisfied with the ratio? If not, make some changes: Reduce the amount of TV you watch, stop bringing as much work home from the office, and scale back other social or sport activities so that you have more time for your teen. Your time and influence are the most powerful protection your teen could have against the effects of the media.

Our Violent Society

According to a 1994 Carnegie Corporation report, nearly one million adolescents between the ages of twelve and nineteen are victimized by violent crime each year. Teenagers are twice as likely to be assaulted as persons aged twenty and older. The rate and intensity of violence involving children has escalated dramatically. The report stated that "The United States has the highest homicide rate of any Western industrialized country—many times higher than the country with the next-highest rate."[8] Much of the violence against adolescents is committed by other adolescents.[9]

William J. Bennett reports in *The Index of Leading Cultural Indicators* that "the fastest-growing segment of the criminal population is our nation's children" and that "because the population group of ten-to-seventeen-year-olds is going to increase significantly in the 1990s, the violent upsurge will probably accelerate."[10] Much of this teenage crime wave includes sexual violence. According to the Bureau of Justice Statistics, "between 1982 and 1991, the arrest rate for juveniles ... for forcible rape [increased] 24 percent ..."[11]

When we start searching for causes of violence in our society, poverty and lack of jobs certainly play a part. But crime is not limited to the poor and jobless.

Experts point to the pervasive influence of violent entertainment. Rap groups sing venom-filled songs about killing police officers and violating women. Video games like *Night Trap* show girls in flimsy night gowns captured by marauders who suck their blood. The popular video game *Mortal Kombat* shows figurines chopping off each others' heads.

Media critics challenge us to ask ourselves serious questions about how we're raising our children. Does a child's love for violence begin when his parents allow him to watch monster cartoons as a preschooler? Is the next logical step for him to watch horror movies and violent programming on TV? Is violent entertainment merely innocent fun or does it anesthetize our sense of the value of life? In fact, does violent entertainment lead to violent action by the viewer?

Columnist William Raspberry claims that the results are in. Reporting on a study by the Center for Research on Aggression at Syracuse University, he states, "Violence on the screen leads to violence in the real world."[12] The director of the center listed three main effects of TV violence uncovered by the studies. The first was an *aggression effect*, which predicts "copycat" violence. In 188 studies involving 244,000 viewers, results showed a substantial number of viewers became more violent after watching violent TV shows. The second was a *victim effect*. Viewers of violent TV were shown to develop an increased level of fearfulness about the world in general. Finally, the *bystander effect* means that people who watch televised violence display an increased degree of callousness and indifference to actual violence, and greater tolerance for higher and higher levels of aggression.[13]

What You Can Do

• *Protect your child against danger.* Teenagers are notorious for experimenting with new and sometimes dangerous people, places, and situations. Your job as a parent is to make sure they understand the dangers and why and how to avoid them. As I've noted elsewhere, try not to sound critical or judgmental when sending this kind of message to your teen. If you do, the message probably won't get through.

• *Keep tabs on your teen's exposure to violent books, comics, music, television programs, or movies.* Pay close attention to the attitudes he is developing toward violence. If you think media violence is having a negative, destructive influence on your child, try substituting less-violent alternatives. Many teens find classic comedies or sports just as entertaining as the media you object to. You'll probably have the greatest success if you use this as an opportunity to find out more about your child's interests.

• *If you think your child may be participating in violent behavior or associating with violent people, it's time to get professional help.* Your challenge will be to keep the lines of communication open as you work at rescuing your child from the world of violence.

• *Teach your children how to be a part of a safer, less violent society*. Show him how to use the Conflict Resolution skills taught in chapter 8. Our teens need to know that fighting and use of force are not acceptable ways of dealing with their feelings of rage or aggression. Research shows that training adolescents in conflict resolution and mediation skills can reduce violence.[14]

Substance Abuse

Alcohol and drug use are almost commonplace aspects of the society we live in. Teenagers feel enormous pressure to go along with the behavior of their peers. Knowing what is happening in the teenage alcohol and drug culture is the first step toward taking preventive measures or solving existing problems. Here are facts you need to know.

Alcohol

• Alcohol-related highway death is the top killer of young people between the ages of fifteen and twenty-four. Over 50 percent of all highway fatalities in a given year are alcohol-related.

• A majority of junior high school students, and more than 90 percent of those in high school, have experimented with alcohol. In one study, 39 percent of the high school students reported participating in binge drinking, defined as five or more drinks in a row.

• Nearly 3.5 million teenagers between the ages of thirteen and seventeen have serious alcohol problems. Almost all of this teen drinking is illegal. Underage drinkers are often supported by their parents' ambivalence about their own drinking habits.

Dick Dutton, director of Alcohol Education for Youth, Inc., and Brian Gleason, coordinator for the Teenage Alcoholism and Alcohol Abuse Rehabilitation Program, wrote the following in an article entitled, "It's Only Booze:"

> A classic cartoon shows a teenager stretched out on a couch, "smashed," with eight or nine empty beer cans on the floor. His parents stand over him and the father says, "Thank God, it's only booze!" Parents have become so terrified of what they know so little about—pot, speed, cocaine and other drugs—that they have missed the increasingly devastating effect of alcohol.[15]

According to Dutton and Gleason, alcohol abuse is America's number-one drug problem. In most communities, drinkers outnumber pot users by at least two to one, and for every heroin addict there are nearly forty-five alcoholics. For young people, alcohol is the drug of choice because of its availability, legality, and cultural acceptability.

Other Drugs

After a decade of decline in drug use by teens, a report released in 1994 sounded an urgent alarm. Researchers from the University of Michigan, who surveyed nearly fifty thousand junior and senior high school students around the country, reported that more teenagers are using marijuana, LSD, inhalants, and stimulants. Commented one researcher,

"It's an early warning to all sectors of society that the improvements of the last decade can't be taken for granted. Each generation of American youth is naive about drugs ..."[16]

Some authorities call the present drug situation an epidemic. Here are some further facts to support that view:

• Among youths between the ages of twelve and seventeen, one in eight tried marijuana within the last month.

• Teenagers almost never try cocaine, crack, or heroin without having first used such "gateway drugs" as tobacco, alcohol, and marijuana.

• Every day five thousand teenagers and adults try cocaine for the first time. According to the National Institute on Drug Abuse, cocaine is a powerfully addictive drug that is dangerous in all forms.

• Drug abuse costs us at least $100 billion annually in criminal activity, medical and legal services, and lost productivity.

• George Beschner, chief of the treatment research branch at the National Institute on Drug Abuse, estimates that multiple drug use has trapped as many as 1.2 million adolescents in America.

• According to one study, the influence of a teen's friends outweighs the influence of family, emotional health, or school problems in the use of drugs.[17]

Why would such potentially damaging and even life-threatening substances appeal to teenagers? Experts point to several deep-seated causes that can produce a craving for drugs: a lack of communication at home, a sense of personal failure and despair, the disintegration of the family, moral laxity, hedonism, and the relentless pressure to perform in a fast-paced society.

What You Can Do:
• *Set a good example.* Abstain from drugs yourself. I know one father who used to enjoy a can of beer at the end of a hard day of work. When his son was born, he decided to abstain from alcohol completely to show that self-control was possible. Even though he faced pressure from friends and family when he decided to stop drinking, he considers the benefits of his example to be greater than the personal satisfaction of having a drink.

You may feel that it's better to teach moderation. Whatever you choose, be sure you're comfortable with the idea of your teen following your example, because he or she probably will.

• *Make sure that you're fully informed.* Read books and articles dealing with drug prevention. The more you know, the better you will handle difficult situations. In a newspaper interview, the mother of a son who had become chemically dependent said, "I wish we'd known what to look for, the signs of chemical dependency. I wish I'd been more aware."[18] Check the Resources section in the back of this book for suggestions.

• *Learn the outward signs of drug use.* Clinical psychologist Charles Hannaford suggests that parents note symptoms in their teens such as the following:

- Changes in behavior, especially becoming overly rebellious
- Changes in clothing styles toward those favored by the drug culture
- Changes in musical tastes, especially a growing interest in heavy metal music
- Declining academic performance
- Frequent outbursts of temper
- Withdrawing from family life
- Being secretive about new friends[19]

• *Tell your teen openly and directly that drug use is not acceptable.* Explain why you're taking that position. Be firm and clear. When you talk, speak your mind, but show your love for your teen. After Time magazine carried a cover story on drugs, a twelve-year-old boy wrote to the editor, "Many young people who run away or feel as if they are not loved turn to drugs. They think it's the only way out."[20] We need to show our teens that it's not.

• *Teach your teen how to say "No."* Practice the "broken record" technique (saying "no thanks" over and over) and the "cold shoulder" routine (simply ignoring the invitation) with your teen. Help your teen or preteen to see resisting peer pressure as a sign of personal strength and victory.

In their book *Drug-Proof Your Kids*, Stephen Arterburn & Jim Burns offer a "Just Say No" game as a way that can teach your teenager to respond to high-pressure situations. It helps teens practice the difficult maneuver of saying no in front of their friends. Take turns working through the examples with your teen.

How should you respond if:

- On a trip to the lake, your older cousin takes you out on a boat ride. When you get to the middle of the lake, he opens a six-pack of beer and reminds you that nobody will ever know.
- At a party, a girl goes into the kitchen to bake some brownies. The rumor circulates that one of the ingredients is marijuana. After ten of your friends have taken one, laughing about how great it is, she offers one to you.
- Your friend's dad offers all of the kids at the party a beer to help them loosen up.
- At one of the local hangouts, a girl offers you a red pill and promises it will make you feel as though you are in another world.
- Before a basketball game, one of the guys on the team says he has a pill that will give everyone super energy so that the team can win.
- At camp, one of the counselors asks you to meet him outside the bunk house after "lights out." You go, thinking it will be a special project or a joke on someone. When you get there, you see that he has a bottle in his hand, and he smells like he has been drinking. He asks you if you would like some.[21]

• *Take aggressive action.* In *How to Get Your Child Off Marijuana*, the Menninger Foundation's Dr. Harold M. Voth advocates taking an aggressive approach to save a child from the consequences of smoking pot. He says that strong action is required when a child is in danger and talking with him about the problem has failed. Dr. Voth advocates three principles for action that apply to other drugs as well as pot. (Because of the seriousness of this kind of intervention, you should only try these actions under the guidance of a professional drug counselor or therapist.)

The first principle is *intervention*. The key to saving your child from marijuana is to interpose yourself between him and the substance for at least three months. If your child denies using marijuana but your suspicions tell you otherwise, then you face a very difficult step: You must simply invade his privacy and carry out a thorough search of his living space and other areas. Very few marijuana smokers are aware of the changes they're making in their lives. This explains why it's so difficult to convince someone to stop.

The second principle is *responsibility*. You, the parent, must temporarily take responsibility for your child's life. Look your child squarely in the eye and tell him clearly and without the slightest equivocation that you are going to take control of the situation in order to stop his use of marijuana.

The third principle is *substitution*. Because marijuana users develop a craving for the drug, parents must find a substitute that can at least satisfy the child's emotional needs. You, the parent, make the best substitute. Although some teens will resist the idea of spending more time with their parents, others will welcome it and find that the time and genuine dialogue they get from you helps fill their needs.[22]

• *Get professional help.* If your son or daughter continues to take drugs and is not responding to your best efforts to deal with the situation, don't wait. Don't let your pride get in your way. Don't deny the seriousness of the problem by saying, "He's just smoking pot; no big deal," or "She's going through a stage; it'll pass." First, look for the best qualified counselor, clinical psychologist, or treatment program you can find. Then join a parents' support group. You'll need all the support, advice, and ideas you can get to face this problem.

• *Don't blame yourself.* If you discover your teen is on drugs, you may experience feelings of guilt, hurt, anger, and helplessness. The sooner you get past blaming your spouse ("You spoiled him!"), yourself ("I should have been more aware!"), or your teen ("How could you do this to us?"), the sooner you can begin to solve the problem.

• *Fight to win.* Face the fact that you are fighting a war ... on drugs. Keep in mind that the enemy is not your teen, it's the drugs. Tell yourself that victory can be the only outcome. Dr. Voth writes that parents need to commit themselves to this challenge with the same kind of intensity soldiers generate when they go into battle. When you save your child's life from drugs, everyone wins.

Sexual Promiscuity and Teen Pregnancy

Someone has said that "a neoconservative is a liberal who has a daughter in high school." That may not be far from the truth. Most parents are very concerned about the safety and health of their teens in a highly charged sexual environment. Adolescents have always faced the challenge of their raging hormones, but today those urges are fueled by a relentless stream of sexually oriented programming and advertising. And today's teens face their temptations without the support of widely accepted moral values.

A national poll of teenagers under seventeen revealed that more than half are sexually active.[23] Here are some additional causes for concern:

• According to one study, three thousand teenage girls in America become pregnant each day. That's a million a year. Four out of five are unmarried. More than half get abortions. As *People* magazine reported, "They are babies having babies. Or killing them."[24]

• A Louis Harris poll indicated that 64 percent of the parents interviewed thought they had little or no control over their teenager's sexual activity and that they needed outside help.

• In response to a request by Ann Landers, eighteen thousand female readers wrote telling of the lines boyfriends use to pressure them into having sex.

"Come on. What are you afraid of? Don't be a baby. It's just part of growing up."

"If you really loved me you would. That's the way people express their true feelings."

"It's very painful for a guy to be in this condition and not get relief."

"I want to marry you someday. We should find out if we are sexually compatible."

"It will be good for your complexion."[25]

• While 10 percent of teenagers marry, the marriages tend to be short-lived. The divorce rate for parents younger than eighteen is three times greater than that of parents who have their first child after age twenty.[26]

• The AIDS virus has created a new urgency behind the need for responsible sex education.

Stories like the following are every parent's nightmare:

> *I'm alone and confused. My boyfriend kept pursuing me for sex ... I had sex with him thinking that I owed it to him.... Later, when I learned I was pregnant, he blew up, told me to get an abortion, and said that it was all my fault. So, to save my parents' heartache and to keep Matt, I had an abortion. Now Matt has left me ...*[27]

Felicia was also a "good kid," who refused to have anything to do with drugs and was careful about whom she dated. She found that Mark shared many of her values and really seemed to care for her. When Felicia lost her virginity to Mark, he told her he had "only been with" two girls in high school. Then, during her senior year in college, she became increasingly fatigued. "Your blood tests confirm you're infected with the AIDS virus," her doctor told her.[28]

Most teenage fathers don't understand how demanding young children can be. When they find out how much time, money, attention, and patience babies demand, they often feel trapped. Groans Carl, aged seventeen:

> *If I'd only known how hard it was going to be, I'd never have let this happen. I thought only about the good times, teaching him to talk and to walk, feeding him every now and then. But he cries all the time, and I have to come up with so much money for his things I can't even afford CDs anymore! I hate my job, and feel like I'll never be able to finish high school.*[29]

Teenage pregnancies cost the nation's taxpayers an estimated $16 billion per year, but the human cost to the hundreds of thousands of teenagers involved is beyond calculation. It would be difficult to overstate this tragedy of lost opportunities and lost happiness.

I believe there are four basic reasons why teenagers face this problem.

First, many teenagers don't know as much about the facts of life as we might think. Unfortunately, teens learn what they know by rumor, on the streets, from firsthand experience, from friends (who have identical sources), or from media such as records, movies, and TV. One pregnant teenager said that her girlfriend told her that you can't get pregnant the first time you have sex!

Second, parents are not talking with their teens about sex ... or listening either. According to psychologist Sol Gordon of Syracuse University, surveys involving more than eight thousand students show that fewer than 15 percent received a meaningful sex education from their parents.[30] Our own survey shows that teens would like to talk with their parents about sexual matters but are afraid their parents will judge them and assume the worse about their behavior.

Third, teens face almost a constant barrage of distorted sexual imagery. The average teenager watches more than four hours of TV daily—more time than he spends doing anything except going to school and sleeping. What does he see? Researchers reported that twenty thousand sexual acts and innuendoes took place on prime-time network television during the course of a year. For four hours a day teens are living in a world where no one ever says premarital sex is wrong, no one ever says no, no one ever gets pregnant, and sexual relationships rarely take place within the context of a healthy, loving marriage.

Finally, most teens haven't developed an adequate moral code—one that would give them good reasons for saying no. They often give in to the passion of the moment because they simply don't know why they shouldn't. According to a study by Josh McDowell, this problem includes teens who attend church with their parents as well as those who don't.

> When I met my boyfriend at the beginning of my sophomore year, we began having sex as soon as we started kissing. I didn't really want to at all—I don't even think he did—but we couldn't think of any reason why we shouldn't do it."[31]

What You Can Do:
• *Show your teen the beauty of fidelity and love within marriage.* When teens ask themselves the question, "Why wait?", they should have a concrete, visual example (yours!) that marriage is worth the wait. If you are a single parent, you still can openly discuss this point with your teen. Point to couples that are happily married as the goal to aim for.

• *Teach your teen that sex within marriage is beautiful.* In their fear of premarital sex, some parents try to tell their teens that sex is dirty and dangerous. But we need to teach them that sex within the context of marriage is enjoyable, satisfying, and fulfilling.

• *Get your facts straight.* Talking to our teens with clarity of purpose and giving accurate information can prevent them from being deceived by the misinformation they'll receive from others. See the Resources section for good books on talking to teenagers about sex.

• *Help your teen develop a positive moral framework.* Since we can't be with our teens every minute, we can't really control their sexual activity. However, we can teach them the moral reasoning behind the rules. If they understand and accept the morality of the situation, they're more likely to police themselves. Make sure they understand that sex is a wonderful gift; that because the urges are powerful and have to do with something as important as the creation of life, sexual expression should be connected to love and commitment in marriage.

• *Be prepared to explain your values regarding sex to your teen.* Your teen will want to know what you think—not only what your values are, but how you arrived at them. Spontaneous discussions may be best. They're often less intimidating than formal "meetings" and make it more likely that your teen will share his true feelings. Brief remarks on your part will give your teen an opportunity to tell you what he needs to talk about.

Linda and Richard Eyre make the point that it is not hypocritical to teach chastity to your teens even when you didn't practice it yourself.[32] One generation's mistakes shouldn't have to be repeated by the next. In fact, many parents have learned that abstinence from sex until marriage is best through their own unfortunate experiences. Aside from the moral and spiritual considerations, the argument for abstinence in terms of the individual's mental, emotional, and physical health and the future stability of their family life is overwhelming.

The daily newspapers provide plenty of opportunity for talking about our values. A few years ago, I found a review that described a current movie as "raucously funny." In the film, a man planned to kill his wife. Before he could carry out his scheme, though, she was kidnapped ... to his great relief and the amusement of the audience. The same paper contained a news account of a man who killed his wife, his two children, and then himself.

We talked to our children about the fact that some people in our society are desperately unhappy, and that some of them try to cover their unhappiness with a sick form of humor, like that in the movie. I also told them, "Children, Mom and I want to assure you that our philosophy of life and our experience in relationships is quite different. There is nothing funny about hate and revenge. Some people laugh at broken relationships because they think laughing is their only alternative. It isn't. It is possible to rebuild relationships through commitment and love."

• *Answer your teen's objections with courage.* Columnist William Raspberry noted that we have "a responsibility not to abdicate fundamental values, even when they are widely ignored. That "everybody is doing it" is in the first place, not true and, in the second, no justification for abandoning our duty to say to the young people under our charge: 'You shouldn't.'"[33]

• *Teach your teen to "Just Say No!"* When ABC Nightline moderator, Ted Koppel, gave a commencement address at Duke University, he declared:

> *"We have actually convinced ourselves that slogans will save us ... Enjoy sex whenever and with whomever you wish, but wear a condom. No! The answer is No. Not because it isn't cool or smart or because you might end up in jail or dying in an AIDS ward, but No because it's wrong ... In its purest form, truth is not a polite tap on the shoulder. It is a howling reproach. What Moses brought down from Mount Sinai were not the Ten Suggestions."[34]*

• *Let's teach our teens that saying no to vice is saying yes to virtue.* Let's teach them that they may need to say no not only to the person they're dating but also to their own feelings and passions. Let's teach them that saying no is a sign of courage and strength, a sign of refusing to let anyone steal their future.

When they've learned why to say no, we can begin to teach them how to say no.

"No. If you really loved me you wouldn't ask."
"I have decided I don't want to have sex before marriage—so don't pressure me."
"I don't care if "everyone's doing it." Sex is not for me until I'm married."

"I respect your feelings and I ask you to respect mine. The answer is no."

"If my 'No' makes you go, that proves I am only a sex object to you. The answer is no."

"Yes, I love you, but I believe a sexual relationship is to be reserved for marriage. My self-respect is too important to settle for second best. If you can't accept my 'No,' that is your problem."

"I know that No now means Yes to a future of self-respect."

• *Explain the practical reasons for chastity.* Stress that abstinence from sex until marriage keeps them free:

- From pregnancy and venereal disease
- From guilt and loss of self respect
- From exploitation by others
- To expand options for personal development
- To develop a range of healthy relationships
- To feel good about themselves

• *Speak openly and directly to your teen.* Many parents feel uncomfortable talking to their teens about sex. Prepare for your talks on this most important subject at least as well as you would for a speech to the PTA or a civic group. Careful planning—sketching out what you want to say and how best to say it—will ensure that you'll get your message across clearly and with a minimum of embarrassment. (Consider how uncomfortable you'll be with the conversations you'll have if your teen isn't properly informed about sex!)

The most effective preparation is to put ourselves in our teen's situation and think, "How would I want my parent to talk to me about sex?" The answer would likely be: cool and relaxed, not hot and bothered; confident, not anxious; firm on principles, not wavering; clear, not ambiguous.

• *Ask for a promise with a ring to it.* In order to do something positive about preparing his adolescent for dating, one father decided to take his son out to dinner on his fifteenth birthday for a "key talk." During their meal he shared his views on chastity and marriage and asked his son to promise to abstain from sex until marriage. As a sign of their agreement, the father gave his son a handsome ring—a visible daily reminder of the commitment he had made. This idea has spread across the country until now thousands of parents are having key talks—mothers with their daughters, fathers with their sons.[35]

• *Don't jump to conclusions.* If your daughter asks, "When a girl misses taking one birth control pill, can she get pregnant?" don't assume she is taking birth control pills, and don't demand anxiously, "Are you pregnant?" That kind of response could make her feel that she isn't trusted and even drive her to the very behavior we fear. She might reason, "Since my mother assumes that I'm having sex, I might as well."

• *Practice forgiveness.* If teens go too far, they need correction and reproof, yes, but they also need your help to rebuild their lives. Be sensitive to their need for love and acceptance and forgiveness. Regardless of how much hurt they may have caused you, if they are sorry, say the actual words "I forgive you" and show acceptance and love in ways that are meaningful to the teen. Use your tone of voice, facial expression, kindness, hugs, and willingness to listen to get your message across.

• *Express your love for your teenager daily.* Teens need to know you love them, or they will look for love in the wrong places. Premarital sex among teenagers is often a problem not of the intellect but of the feelings. Some feel a tremendous need for love and acceptance and are willing to trade their bodies to get it. Passions are easier to control when parents see that their teen's basic emotional needs are met.

Teen Suicide

No parent ever gets used to reports like the following:

Alsip, IL. (AP)—Two young women, one holding a rose and a stuffed animal, the other a photo album, were found dead in a garage, apparently victims of the same method of suicide used by four teenagers in New Jersey, police said yesterday.[36]

Dr. R. John Kinkel, reporting on teen suicide to the American Psychiatric Association, said that people have underestimated the prevalence of teen suicide. Nearly eight out of one hundred U.S. teenagers attempt suicide every year, far more than experts had previously believed.

The results of his study of nearly three thousand adolescents (the largest ever done on the subject in the U.S.) closely links suicide attempts to drug and alcohol use. He also found that suicide attempts were twice as common among females, the most vulnerable being between the ages of fourteen and sixteen and a half. Here are some more details on this horrible epidemic.

• During the last decade, the suicide rate in the fifteen-to-nineteen-year-old bracket has gone up over 400 percent. In one year over six hundred thousand American teens attempted to take their lives.

• According to the National Center for Health Statistics, the rate at which teenagers are taking their own lives has more than tripled since 1960.[37]

• Suicide ranks as the third-most-common killer of teens—behind accidents and homicides. Some experts think a good number of accidents may actually be suicides.[38]

• Of five hundred teenagers who responded to a magazine survey, 73 percent said they have thought about committing suicide, and 70 percent said they knew someone who had attempted suicide.[39]

• The reason most often given for contemplating suicide was "not getting along with parents," followed by a fear of not being able to live up to other people's expectations. Loneliness, problems with relationships, and concern about appearance were also mentioned as major reasons.[40]

• About a quarter of the teens in this survey said they have no one they can talk to about their suicidal thoughts; 15 percent said they don't think their problems are important enough to talk about.[41]

In a guest editorial in *USA Today*, Richard Krawiec wrote, "Suicide is a desperate scream, a final attempt to communicate how [teenagers] feel about life and the world they inhabit."[42] It is a tragic message, a struggle to be heard in a world that doesn't seem to be listening. Parents, stunned by the recent rise in teen suicides, realize they cannot arrogantly assume "This will never happen to my child."

What causes a teen to attempt suicide? In addition to drugs and alcohol, experts think contributing factors include premature sexual involvements, family crises, depression, loneliness, rejection, lack of communication, poor self-image, unrelieved stress, and a feeling of not meeting expectations and standards. Sometimes there are no apparent answers—only questions.

A teen's words and actions are clues that can alert parents to the possibility of a teen's suicidal tendencies. Spoken clues can range from direct and dramatic statements such as "I might as well kill myself," or "I suppose you would be happier if I weren't around anymore," to "Nothing matters; it's no use." Behavioral clues might include a prolonged depression, signs of despair, disorientation, and panic, or acts of self-destruction through alcoholism, drug abuse, or reckless driving.

Stressful events such as the divorce of parents, failing a final exam, being rejected by a girlfriend/boyfriend, and the death of a parent, grandparent, friend, or pet can also increase the risk.

Some teens may find reinforcement for their suicidal feelings in certain rock music. "Suicidal Failure," from the album *Suicidal Tendencies*, presents this outlook on life:

> *Father forgive me*
> *For I know now what I do;*
> *I tried everything*
> *Now I'll leave it up to you.*
> *I don't want to live.*
> *I don't know why.*
> *I don't have no reasons,*
> *I just want to die.*[43]

And here are the lyrics to "Suicide Solution":

> *Breaking laws, knocking doors,*
> *But there's no one at home.*
> *Made your bed, rest your head,*
> *But you lie there and moan.*
> *Where to hide, suicide*
> *Is the only way out*
> *Don't you know what it's really about?*[44]

Although the writer claims the song is really about alcohol (suicide *solution*), the lyrics have been blamed as contributing to the death of John McCollum, aged nineteen, who apparently committed suicide after listening to "Suicide Solution" for five hours. Understandably, John McCollum's family doesn't think that the lyrics are about alcohol.

Another teenager, Steve Boucher, is reported to have shot himself in the head while listening to the song, "Shoot to Thrill" by another heavy metal group.

> *Shoot to thrill,*
> *Way to kill,*
> *I got my gun at the ready,*
> *Gonna fire at will.*[45]

What kind of influence do lyrics like these have on teenage suicides? We don't know for sure, but it may be greater than most parents realize.

When teens turn to lyrics that reinforce their despair, or other clues alert us to the fact that something is very wrong, what can we do? What can we say? Parents often have no idea of what they should do and are afraid they'll make matters worse.

What You Can Do:

• *Get professional help.* If you suspect that your teenager may be suicidal, contact a qualified counselor or psychologist immediately. The risks are too high for you to try to work things out on your own. (Also, consult the Resources section in the back of this book.)

• *Listen hard.* Because of the unique role they play in their children's lives, parents can release an awesome healing power when they choose to practice deep and active listening. Force yourself not to comment on or contradict your teen's negative statements. If your teen says, "Life is meaningless!" don't say "That's a terrible thing to say!" Instead, echo their feelings with a statement like, "Life must look pretty awful to you right now," and then listen. Your goal is to keep the channels of communication open. Teenagers often feel some relief if they can vent their feelings through talking.

• *Take the initiative.* A depressed teenager may want to talk but not know how to begin. Don't be afraid to be direct. "I've noticed that you seem troubled lately. Let's talk about it. I'm ready to listen." Or come right out and ask, "Are you happy?" If your teen says "No," do your best to find out why.

• *Demonstrate your unconditional love for your teen.* Even when our teens seem to be doing everything possible to drive us away, we need to let them know that they can count on our love for them as persons. We must never let them think that any failure or embarrassment that they may have brought into the family will lead to their loss of our love.

• *Teach your teen coping skills.* We need to talk to our teens about how we have learned to handle the bumps and bruises of everyday life. Many teens are so focused on what happened today that they need help in developing a broader perspective on what's going on in their lives. Just knowing that everyone suffers from ups and downs and that it is possible to survive the failures and stress of everyday life can help.

I once tried to demonstrate this point to our children by telling them how I felt when a college girlfriend broke up with me. We laughed as I described kicking a telephone pole in anger and then hopping around howling in pain. I explained that now I feel that the break-up was the best thing that ever happened to me, even though at the time it seemed like the worst. If it hadn't been for that painful break-up, I would never have met their mother!

• *Talk to your teen about their options.* Suicide occurs because young people feel it is their only option. We must help them to see—not just by words, but by our examples—that life is worth living, that there is more than one way to deal with problems, that we will help them learn to solve the problems they face, that we really are on their team. We must help them to realize that they will survive the mood swings and depressive fits of adolescence, that their mistakes and failures are not the only measures of their worth, and that the great part of being human is our capacity to start over again.

Disaffection and Despair among the Slacker Generation

When President Clinton appeared on MTV in 1994 to find out what was on the minds of America's youth, he must have been troubled by what he heard. As a *New York Times* reporter related, "A streak of nihilism ran through many of the questions."[46]

Typical was a question from seventeen-year-old Dahlia Schweitzer, who wanted to know what the President thought about the suicide of Kurt Cobain, lead singer of the rock group Nirvana. The teenager suggested that the self-destruction of the singer "exemplified the emptiness that many in our generation feel, the lack of importance we place on life." Then she asked, "How do you propose to change this mentality?"[47]

The President didn't really know what to say. Perhaps he was as lost as many parents are when it comes to dealing with this kind of mentality. Just what are these teenagers thinking? And what, if anything, can we do about it?

Some commentators have tried to describe Generation X (eighteen-to-twenty-nine-year-olds) as a group of slackers, whiners, and complainers. An article in Esquire called them "The New Lost Generation." But after studying the issue, the Roper Center stated: "Our extensive research shows there are no significant national or personal mood differences separating young and old."[48] The Center found that while 25 percent of the twenty-somethings polled said that they were unhappy with their lot in life, 26 percent of the baby-boomers said the same thing.[49]

It appears clear that what we might call the "slacker attitude" cannot be tied to any one generation. There have always been those who could be described as "beat," "tuned out," "lost," or just plain bored. If your adolescent is part of the 25 percent who are dissatisfied with life, though, these percentages and labels are not much consolation. As parents, we want to understand the problem better so that we can help our teens solve it.

How would you describe the attitude of your teen or older adolescent? Put a check mark by the following descriptions if your teen demonstrates:

_____ persistent unhappiness
_____ lack of interest in anything
_____ scorn for the past
_____ dogged dissatisfaction with the present
_____ confusion or lack of concern about the future
_____ a lack of meaning or purpose
_____ a sense that society owes her something
_____ self-hatred or a poor self-concept
_____ lack of interest in work (or, if not in school: unemployed or underemployed)
_____ explosive anguish or rage
_____ a sense of victimization by society, others, etc.
_____ few or no friends, or superficial relationships

If you checked two or more of these characteristics, you should pay special attention to this section. It's possible that in your teen's case the symptoms are only temporary by-products of typical adolescent turmoil. If so, time and caring communication will help ease the pain. But it is also possible that such symptoms represent a more persistent combination of attitudes, beliefs, and feelings that can cripple your teen's drive toward maturity and independence.

In that case, you'll need to make a more drastic effort to help your teen change his or her attitudes. There are no easy solutions, but here are some options that may help.

What You Can Do:
• *Find ways to help your teen develop more positive beliefs.* Opinions, thoughts, and beliefs make up a significant part of the "slacker attitude." Many teens develop a near-nihilistic sense that there is no meaning or purpose to their existence. Ask yourself the following questions:

- "Does my adolescent's unhealthy beliefs reflect those of his friends? If so, what steps can I take to help him make new friends in order to balance the influence of the old?" A few possibilities: You could encourage your teen to change schools, join a youth group, attend a summer camp, or invite new acquaintances to your home for a dinner or party.
- "Does my adolescent have a religious faith? Is that faith vital, real, and genuine, or is it more of a routine? What can I do about it?" You might want to try attending church with your teen. Or try a different church or synagogue that might provide a welcome change of scenery. You can also provide inspirational books, such as C. S. Lewis's *Mere Christianity* or Rabbi Harold Kushner's *Who Needs God?* (See the Resources section at the back of this book for other possibilities.)
- "Does my adolescent have a sense of purpose or meaning in life? If not, what can I do to help her find it?" Try talking to your teen about how you found your own purpose in life. This could also be a good opportunity to refocus on your own goals and purposes. A number of books provide excellent discussions of this process—for example, Victor Frankl's *Man's Search for Meaning* or Richard N. Bolles's *How to Find Your Mission in Life.*
- "Does my adolescent read, listen to, or watch media that reflect a disaffected or despairing attitude?" If so, take a second look at the discussion of media influences at the beginning of this chapter, and take the appropriate steps. Encourage your teen to read character-building stories like those in William J. Bennett's *The Book of Virtues* or

even classic self-help books such as Norman Vincent Peale's *The Power of Positive Thinking* and Dale Carnegie's *How to Win Friends and Influence People*. It may be difficult, but try to get your teen at least to sample movies or videos with uplifting messages that could leave him with renewed compassion, a sense of challenge, a model of courage and hope, or an expanded view of the world. Remember the proverb, "As a person thinks in his heart, so is he" (Proverbs 23:7).

- "Does my teen participate in positive, life-affirming activities?" You can try to involve your teen in activities that will broaden his horizons, teach him the value of human life, and affect his attitudes. At this writing, for example, our children Jud and Jessica have just returned from a "High Road Adventure"—two weeks in the wilderness in upper Wisconsin. What difference did it make? They both shared a new sense of the value of life, the thrill of surviving hardships, the significance of working together to get a job done, the joy of friendship, and a deeper appreciation for their parents. My impression is that the experience will have a life-long impact on their attitudes.

With adolescents in their late teens or twenty-somethings, consider doing volunteer work together. This could include driving for "Meals on Wheels," tutoring deprived children, or helping distribute food or clothing to the homeless. The idea is to help break your teen's self-preoccupation by introducing her to people with particularly acute problems and showing her the joy of helping the less fortunate. This could require a real effort on your part, but the benefits would last a lifetime.

• *Listen carefully to your teen's feelings.* Feelings are like a freight train—they have a momentum that may take a while to stop. Nor is it easy to change their direction. But feelings are the "freight cars" of the train, not the "engine." Our feelings are driven by our thoughts, and thoughts can more easily be directed.

The process of healing requires that emotions be brought out in the open. That process is not always pleasant. In fact, some of the feelings your teen voices will seem unpleasant or unfair. But right or wrong, they cannot be cured if they are hidden away in a corner of your teen's mind.

Listen carefully and in a nonjudgmental way to the negative emotions your adolescent expresses. The ACE listening skills discussed earlier in the book can be a powerful tool. Here is another example of effective and ineffective ways of dealing with a teen's emotional turmoil:

Emotional Event: Teen watching TV and obviously unhappy.

Ineffective Listening

You: What are you moping about?

Teen: Life stinks!

You: I don't understand your generation. You've never had to fight a war or even dodge one like I did. You have everything a kid could want. What more do you expect?

Teen: I expect a lot more. I expect a life, not just a meaningless job like the one you have. I expect that life ought to be fun—worth getting up for in the morning. I expect people to treat me like I was somebody, not a bag of scum.

You: You know what I think? I think you think too much. I think you want life handed to you on a silver platter. I think you ought to get off your butt and earn some money instead of crying about everything.

Teen: I don't care what you think!

Effective Listening

You: You seem troubled. What are you feeling?

Teen: Life stinks!

You: You're unhappy with your situation in life.

Teen: Yes, I've tried to get a job, but nothing is available.

You: You've knocked on doors, but none of them budge. What kind of job are you looking for?

Teen: I don't really know what I want to do ...

You: I see.

Teen: I want to be happy in what I'm doing. Is that too much to ask?

You: That's certainly reasonable. I suppose most people want that ...

Teen: Okay, so what do I do?

You: Have you ever taken the Strong Vocational Interest test?

Teen: No. What is it?

You: It identifies what your interests are and then shows you how your interests match up with others who are successful in various field of work.

Teen: I don't think it will help. I know what my interests are and I've looked into various jobs. Nothing clicks.

Notice that the problem hasn't been fully resolved. But the parent and teen are talking and listening to each other—starting to move out of the rut of unhealthy feelings. Obviously, this process is likely to take a lot of work and a great deal of time. But our teen's feelings of frustration, failed expectations, and social rejection can often be relieved through careful, empathetic listening.

It's possible that you'll need professional help. But in any case, your listening skills are vital. Take the time to hear your teen out. If you have to miss your favorite soap opera or a football game, do it. If your teen wants to talk and you have to stay up till 1:00 A.M., do it. Be there for your teen.

Let's keep in mind that at some point our teens are responsible for their own attitudes. Especially with older adolescents, there may be little that we can do. But when the window of opportunity opens, let's teach our teens to express their feelings freely and to respond positively to life.

Action Steps for Confronting Major Problems

Throughout this chapter I've suggested a number of practical things you can do to deal with the major crises you may face with your teen. Here I'd like to add some general advice that should help any parent/teen relationship.

• *Give your teen something to believe in.* This is a life-long process that must start long before the teenage years. It requires that you know what you believe, that your philosophy is adequate to life's demands, that you clearly express your beliefs to your children, and that you act and talk in ways consistent with your deepest beliefs.

• *Speak the truth in love.* If a conflict arises over rules or boundaries, use the Conflict Resolution Model to state your opinion. Be flexible when you can be and admit insufficient knowledge when necessary, but be firm when you have to be. The firmness of caring communication is really an exercise in love.

• *Build trust in your judgment.* Keep in mind that just because some rock lyrics are unacceptably violent or lewd doesn't mean that all rock music is unacceptable. And that just because some TV shows are unacceptably violent doesn't mean that they all are.

After giving a presentation to hundreds of teens on MTV, media specialist Quentin Schultze found himself counseling a long line of disgruntled youth. They agreed with his argument that MTV often presented a nihilistic and selfish view of life. They were upset, however, that their parents had hastily rejected the channel without considering that not all rock videos are evil. Their parents' oversimplification of the situation had reduced the teens' trust in their parent's judgment.[50]

• *Write messages to your teenager.* Talking face to face about problems can be very difficult, especially when emotions run high. We may communicate much better by taking the time to think through what we really want to say and writing it down. As we read what we have written, we can ask ourselves, "Is this what I really want to say? Is it fair? Does it convey not only my concern or disagreement, but also my love and support?"

• *Take advantage of the power of positive networking.* Many families cannot survive the pressures of our society without the help of friends who care and are willing to be mutually supportive. In the ups and downs of parenting, my family has gained tremendous support and long-term positive influence from youth advisers, teachers, adult role models, and peers of our children who were committed to similar values.

• *Speak up for yourself.* If you are suffering because your teen has made some wrong choices, don't panic. Go to a pastor, counselor, or friend with whom you can be completely honest, and unburden your heart. If you are religious, take advantage of the healing power of prayer.

• *Don't panic.* Keep in mind that you have prepared for this battle by investing ten or twelve or more years of your life in raising your children. In most cases, teens are loyal to their family and want things to work out for the best. If you can show your teen that you're trying to understand them—that you want to see their point of view as well as your own—the battle is more than half won. Never give up!

CHAPTER TWELVE

THE FIVE MESSAGES TEENS WANT TO HEAR

BY JUDSON SWETS

I hate to say it, but my parents don't talk much to me or it's the other way around. We're just like animals not knowing how to speak or show emotion. I don't blame my parents or myself, because that's the way we were raised. But in future, I hope our communication will be better.

— JANE, AGE 17

Dad has always wanted to involve the family in his projects. One of his favorite daydreams was to use the entire family to prepare his books in the living room for mail order ... in full assembly-line fashion. As a result, I was not surprised when Dad asked me, a fledgling teenager, to help him write this book.

"Sure, Dad, I'll write a chapter," I said offhandedly, "but don't forget, I'm ahead five games to four. Your serve." Little did I know how involved this project would later become.

In preparing this chapter, I wanted to use my "teenagerness" to give you a new perspective on the special communication needs of teenagers. To make sure that I wasn't just speaking for myself, I based this chapter on eight hundred responses I received from a survey of my peers. I asked junior and senior high school students, "If you could choose what your parents tell you, what would you want them to say?" Some of their responses were quite creative:

"Don't study tonight. Just have fun."

"We'll buy you a car when you're sixteen ... and pay for the insurance."

"You don't have to take out the garbage anymore."

"Here's that $500 you wanted."

"Since you're too tired to get up, I'll have your brother do your chores."

"I love it when your room is messy!"

Next I asked, "What do your parents actually tell you on a daily basis?" Some of the responses I received reflect the daily conflicts that can make home life such a hassle.

"You had better get good grades or you will mess up your entire life!"

"You're grounded for a month! ... Make that two months!"

"No TV for a week. Go to your room and study."

"I don't care if everyone else does it. If 'everyone' jumped off the Empire State Building, would you?"

"When I was your age ..."

"Where are you going? With whom? Who's driving? Remember your curfew. Wear your seat belt. Be careful!"

"You've been on the phone for five minutes! Get off the phone!"

"Because I said so, and that's final!"

Even teenagers agree that communication at home can be better than this.

Throughout the responses, I found five distinct "messages" that were repeated again and again. In the following pages, I'll describe in detail the five messages that most teens—and probably your teen—want to hear.

1. "I'm proud of you."

This phrase helps build a teenager's self-esteem. It is generally associated with achievement, but a teen will need to hear this statement more when he fails than when he succeeds. My father often says, "Son, do you know I am proud of you no matter what?" The word "proud" in this context is closely related to love. I know it means that my father is happy I am his son.

Do you remember how good it felt when your parents or a teacher would say, "I'm proud of you"? The good feeling their approval gave you probably made a lasting impression. Or maybe you rarely heard your parents express appreciation for your appearance or behavior or accomplishments. Apparently, many teens today do not hear this message.

> *"I wish my parents would just tell me they're proud of me instead of always being so hard on me. It seems like I never do anything right, and when I do, they tell me I could have done better."*
> — CHARLA (16)

> *"I wish that when I bring home good grades, ribbons, or awards, they would tell me that they are proud of me."*
> — BRIAN (17)

> *"I want to hear them say that I am a great daughter, that I'm just what they wanted, that they are proud of me."*
> — SUE (13)

All of these teenagers are looking to their parents to fill their need for approval. Ever since we were old enough to remember, we have sought the praise of our parents. After a preschooler draws a picture, he runs to his mommy for approval. If an elementary school student makes an A on a test, she is sure to tell Mom and Dad about it because their approval is important.

Parents have to be careful not to set their standards for their teenagers too high. If teens think that they have to make all A's to be accepted by their parents, they may feel that their parents are only concerned about success and not about them as persons. As a result, they may not try to do their best. This may be why some teens with superior abilities do just enough to get by.

I think that parents should express appreciation to their teens for what they are and the genuine efforts they make—not comparing them to others or setting up an arbitrary standard such as, "You must make all A's." Pride in one's child shouldn't depend on points scored, grades earned, or gaining admittance to a socially elite group.

"I'm proud of you" should be said any time teenagers:

- Choose to put in an extra effort to achieve a personal goal

- Choose to overcome peer pressure and make their own decisions
- Determine to learn from their mistakes and try again
- Use their natural abilities to the fullest

Teens want to build a general bank account of approval based on who they are as persons, not on their daily performances. Then when they fail, they can draw from that bank for self-esteem. If teens don't get the approval they crave from their parents, they may begin to look for it in all the wrong places.

In his book, *How to Make Your Child a Winner*, Dr. Victor B. Cline says that kids are lazy because their parents permit it.[1] I believe this is true. Motivating your child is an important part of your job as a parent. For example, you can influence a younger child to practice piano for fifteen minutes every day. When the child plays his first piece, you'll be proud of him, even though you had to work to make him persevere long enough to learn the piece. Your child's sense of accomplishment, triggered by your approval, will help him build the inner desire that will eventually cause him to become self-motivated.

This same strategy can be applied to teenagers. Parents who retain their authority have the power to influence their teens' actions. Through the careful use of their parental authority, discipline, and positive motivation, parents must try to develop positive qualities and a sense of achievement in their teens. When it works, they can say to their teen, as if he or she had done all the work alone, "I'm proud of you."

It can be difficult to be proud of our teens when they make wrong decisions or fail to do their best. However, you should never, never, withhold love.

When a teen fails, don't say, "You will never amount to anything." A simple slip of the tongue like that can really hurt. In effect it says, "I'm disappointed in you as a human being." Such thoughts crush self-esteem and carry a sense of permanence that can snuff out the motivation needed to strive for improvement.

Generally, the feeling of being loved is needed more during times of failure than during times of success. Parents need to accept teens when they fail so that they can rebuild their confidence and try again. Try to keep this distinction in mind: you can still accept the person even when you can't approve the behavior. Although an "I'm proud of you" message may be inappropriate, you can still affirm your teenager as a person. Make it plain by what you say that it is only their actions that disappoint you.

Your "I'm proud of you" message will encourage your teenager to set higher goals and fuel his desire to reach those aims. It will raise his self-esteem and give him the confidence he needs.

2. "You can come to me with anything and I'll always be there to listen."

Teenagers consider this message important because it assures them that when there is a problem or misunderstanding, the first and hardest step can be taken—they can come to their parents and get a hearing. A parent's failure to listen is a major reason teens keep to themselves. Parents often fall into negative attention habits without knowing it. Then they miss an awful lot that could have been said:

> *"If I knew my parents would really listen to me, I would tell them how much I love them and appreciate them. I would tell them that I know they work hard to get me some of the things I want. I would also tell them that when I graduate and move out, I will never forget what they have done for me."*
>
> — BRIAN (15)

> *"If my parents would listen to me, I would tell them all my problems and tell them how I feel. I would also tell them that I rely on them to listen to my problems and to help me solve them."*
>
> — BRANDON (12)

> *"I want my parents to take the time to listen to me like they would to a good friend. I would tell them that I am sorry for any pain that I have caused them and that I love them. I would tell them that I would do anything in the world for them."*
>
> — MELINDA (16)

In chapter 4 you read about how to "Earn the Right to be Heard." I call the following basic rules of listening how to "Earn the Right to be Told."

The responses from the survey suggest that these rules are essential to getting your teens to talk to you. They underscore the kind of listening that teenagers expect from their parents.

• *Give your undivided attention.* This means you should stop cooking, stop reading the newspaper or watching TV, stop thinking about other things, and concentrate on what your teen says.

• *Do not talk when you are trying to listen.* A good listener is not always talking. Empathy is sometimes best communicated by intentional silence and focused attention.

• *Be fully present.* Teens want parents who will "be there" for them when they go through their most difficult times.

• *Be open-minded.* Teens want parents who will not ridicule them even though their ideas are maybe crazy or not well thought out. They want parents who will try to focus on what it's like to be thirteen or fifteen and not on what an idea sounds like from the perspective of maturity.

• *Listen with a willingness to understand.* Make it your goal to completely understand your teen, and focus on reaching that goal.

When you listen in this way, you communicate powerful uplifting messages without saying a word:

"You are important to me."

"I care about the things you are interested in."

"I enjoy listening to your thoughts, ideas, and opinions."

"I love you."

Good listening also increases your teen's willingness to talk. It builds mutual respect and trust. Saying, "You can come to me with anything ..." not only strengthens your relationship but sets the foundation for keeping it going even in your most difficult moments.

When you improve your own active listening skills, your teen will learn to listen better. Imagine the positive impact that would have on the quality of conversation in your home.

3. *"I want to understand you."*

Patty wrote this about her mother:

"I don't think she would understand my personal problems because she is so much older than I and probably has forgotten what it was like when she was a teen."

— PATTY (15)

It must be frustrating to be a parent. You hear our prejudices about the "generation gap." You sense that sometimes we accuse you of not understanding as a way of building our own defenses. You discover that sometimes we equate understanding with agreement. No wonder it's difficult to communicate with us.

Parents, don't let your teenagers manipulate you. If you are charged with not understanding, ask your teen to help you understand. Tell your teen, "I want to understand. Tell me more. What are you feeling?"

If you think you just disagree with your teen, restate what he has said to his satisfaction and then repeat your views. You may need to say, "I think I understand what you want to do and why you want to do it. If I don't, I want to understand you. But it seems to me that our problem is not one of misunderstanding but of disagreement."

Although each teenager is unique, all seem to share certain unhappy emotions, feelings of frustration, failure, inferiority, loneliness, non-acceptance, and being unloved. Try to identify the emotion as well as you can and then ask if your guess is accurate. Say, "Are you feeling frustrated?" or "I understand that you might be feeling not accepted—is that right?"

If you don't have it quite right, but maintain an openness to your teen, she will likely try to help you target the emotion. If it is a matter of not being able to identify with how your teen feels, she will at least know that you are trying your best to understand.

This process will not only increase your understanding of the situation, it will communicates something more—that you cared enough to try, to hang in there, to do the sometimes unpleasant work of seeing conflict through to a happy solution ... or at least to a resolution both you and your teen can live with.

Warning! Never say, "I understand exactly how you feel!" It sounds like you are discounting our feelings or trying for a quick solution to a problem. We are likely to respond, "Oh, no, you don't. You are not me. You don't know the whole story. You can't possibly understand exactly how I feel!"

I think it's helpful to aim at three goals when trying to understand your teen:

- Make sure that your teen understands that you want to understand.
- Take the time to discover the motives behind your teen's statements or requests before forming an opinion.

- Listen with empathy, remembering how you felt when you were a teen.

4. *"I trust you."*

Having the trust of parents is important to many teens:

"The most damaging thing my parents ever said to me was when they told me they could never trust me again."
— PAM (18)

"I wish my mom would put some trust in me and tell me that she trusts me, has faith in me, and thinks that I sometimes act responsibly instead of telling me I'm always irresponsible and immature."
— KRIS (14)

One good reason parents are afraid to convey trust is because their teens have taken advantage of them in the past. A student who would not sign his name on the survey wrote,

"I will say to my parents, 'Will you please trust me on this,' and then I will go out and do the thing I told them to trust me not to do."

Not everyone agrees. Susan wrote,

"I have my own morals and standards and I tell my parents what I do, even when I think they might disagree. We talk about it and usually work things out. I need my parents' trust in order to believe in myself."
— SUSAN (17)

Teens need you to tell them that your trust in them will develop gradually as they acquire knowledge and experience in situations that require trust. You simply would not trust your thirteen-year-old to drive your new car because, aside from its being illegal, he would not have the experience necessary to allow you to trust his judgment.

But I suspect there is another reason it's hard for parents to trust teens as much as they'd like. Parents know themselves. They have surely experienced the forces of temptation firsthand, and they know how easy it is to yield to negative pressure when you're not ready for it. This prevents parents from giving their children unlimited trust. In fact, parents would not be doing their jobs if they allowed their child to enter situations where the degree of temptation was higher than that child's level of maturity.

Suppose there is a disagreement about curfew. If the teen says, "Don't you trust me?", the parent faces a dilemma. He doesn't want to say "No" and yet he can't say "Yes." A more reasonable response would sound something like this: "Son, I do trust your intentions, but staying out past curfew increases the temptations you face. I would not be doing my job as a parent if I allowed you to be in a situation where the temptations are greater than you can handle."

The trick is to achieve some kind of balance. Some degree of trust must be given in order for that trust to be proven. Teenagers also need a second chance (not necessarily without consequences) when they have failed and are truly sorry. Say "I trust you" whenever you can. When my parents say it to me, it makes me want to live up to their trust.

5. "I love you."

In his book *Reality Therapy*, Dr. William Glasser breaks down the causes of mental illness into the frustration of two basic needs: the need to love and the need to be loved.[2] In spite of the great importance of these needs, parents sometimes miss opportunities to express love—as well as receive it—because they've forgotten to make the communication of love a conscious goal. Yet, according to our survey, guys as well as girls rated this the most important message they want to hear from their parents.

> *"I wish my parents would say to me every day, not just every other day, that they love me and that they are proud of me."*
> — KEN (13)

> *"I wish my dad would say, "I love you," more. I think he thinks I'd be embarrassed if my friends heard him, but I definitely would not."*
> — SUSAN (17)

> *"I want to hear that they will always love me no matter how I do in life, whether I succeed or fail."*
> — BRIAN (15)

"I would like to hear that my dad loves me. He never tells me that. It hurts when your own parents don't tell you that they love you. When I have children, I will tell them I love them even when I punish them or even when they make mistakes. I would tell them that I also make mistakes and that I am not perfect."

— DAVID (14)

Love is the essential ingredient in healthy family relationships. "I love you"—said out loud and often—helps us know who we are and why we were born. When an adolescent is not sure of parental love, the other four messages don't mean anything. Teens need to feel love communicated and demonstrated. How can teens be certain that they are loved if they are never told? How can teens feel certain that they are loved if their parents never spend time with them?

Some parents may think that they show love through material gifts. They may find a sense of satisfaction in giving these gifts, but then become hurt when their teens don't show gratitude or seem satisfied. The problem might be that what seems like a clear expression of love to the parent may be viewed by the teen as a substitute for love. A son may prefer that his dad take the time to go fishing with him, instead of buying him a new fishing pole. A daughter may prefer that her mother relax, sit down at the kitchen table, and just talk instead of having her rush off to buy the latest fashions. The way to demonstrate love to your teenagers is spelled T-I-M-E.

Giving your teen material gifts, providing food and shelter, showing them respect in a thousand ways still isn't adequate. Words by themselves are not enough. You also need to show evidence of your willingness to spend time with your adolescent; to go on fishing trips, to go shopping together, to take the time to fully listen.

One of the classic expressions of the full dimensions of love is contained in Saint Paul's first epistle to the Corinthians:

Love is patient, love is kind ... It is not rude, it is not self-seeking, it is not easily angered, it keeps no record of wrongs ... It always protects, always trusts, always hopes, always perseveres (I CORINTHIANS 13:4,5,7).

Perhaps you've heard those words many times before. But take a minute to reflect on them now from an adolescent's perspective.

Patience is letting your teen finish saying what's on his mind. It's not getting angry at unintended mistakes. It's allowing your teen the time needed to grow up.

Kindness is talking and listening to your teen the way you would to your best friend. It shows in your smile. It's clearly conveyed in your eyes. It results from empathy.

Not being rude means providing common courtesy. It's refusing to yell, call your teen names, or engage in put-downs. Not being easily angered means being firm when necessary without being insulting. It's caring enough to exercise self-control. It's remembering one's own mistakes.

Keeping no record of wrongs means not bombarding your teen with reminders of past mistakes. It means forgiving and forgetting.

Protecting means setting boundaries, instilling virtues, and building character.

Trusting means giving the freedom to make mistakes and the encouragement to start afresh.

Hoping means acting with unconditional love even when it's not deserved.

Persevering means hanging tough as a parent until the job is done.

As you can see, the first four messages are important, but they're based on your love for your teenager. All five messages are important to teenagers, but the greatest is love.

Listening to what your teens tell you and treating their concerns as legitimate and important are essential parts of building the kind of relationship you want. You should treat them as you expect to be treated. How can you expect them to take your pleas for maturity, responsibility, and communication seriously if you ignore their requests for support, approval, and trust? If you do listen, you'll find that you can develop a powerful and motivated ally in keeping the lines of communication open.

Relationships take work. This is true in marriage, friendship, and parenting. The parent/teen relationship may take even more effort because it constantly changes as the teen grows older and gains more independence. This transition to adulthood can be a rocky one, and it is easy for parents to become frustrated and stop working at the relationship.

Don't let this happen in your family. Teens need parents during the adolescent years as much as ever. They need to hear that you are proud of them, that you will always be there to listen, that you want to understand them, that you trust them, and most importantly, that you love them.

WORDS OF
ENCOURAGEMENT

Life is an adventure in forgiveness.
　　　　　　— NORMAN COUSINS, *Human Options*[1]

Early on during the process of writing this book I felt discouraged by the feeling that I wasn't making any headway.
Since I had planned the book as a joint project with my son,
I decided to discuss the matter with him. According to my journal
entry, our conversation went like this:

Me:　Jud, the writing is not going well. Do you think I should
　　　　give it up?
Jud:　Well, Dad … I know you may be feeling bad that you
　　　　haven't made more progress. It's like your mind is in a traf-
　　　　fic jam. There are too many things you have to do right now.
　　　　When the traffic clears, you'll be able to write again.
Me:　Hmmm … that's a nice thought.
Jud:　Besides, did you ever feel this way when you were writ-
　　　　ing your first book?
Me:　Yes, several times.
Jud:　OK, then you know you can get over this obstacle, too!

　　I felt *encouraged*.
　　Another time I was angry and expressed it to the family. I
don't remember what the problem was, but I have in front of me
a letter written that evening by my daughter, who at that time was
about twelve:

Dear Dad,

Remember the "Super Dad" poem I wrote for you? You are a super dad. And nobody likes it when you are mad, not even you. I LOVE YOU! I hope you feel better soon.

Love, Jessica

P.S. I have a hug for you when you want one.

I felt *forgiven.*

It is my hope that this book *encourages* you as much as these responses from my children encouraged me ... for no one needs encouragement more than the parents of teenagers. Teenagers can present special problems, and no one is bruise proof, especially not parents. As Shakespeare said, "How sharper than a serpent's tooth it is to have a thankless child."[2]

You may have been hurt by things your children have said or done. When teenagers seem thankless, when they take their adolescent turmoil out on us, when they skillfully make us feel inadequate, or that we have failed, we hurt. When they hurt themselves through their inexperience or inappropriate behavior, we hurt.

But regardless of how downcast or upset we might feel at times, pessimism or cynicism or surrender are not really options. The prodigal son or daughter may yet come home. We don't know enough about the future to be pessimistic.

Let's focus on what we do know. We know that our children are gifts from God. And we know that their adolescence will create great challenges and strains on relationships—for them and for us. Parenting adolescents is like climbing the rough side of a mountain. Sometimes we take one step forward and slip two steps back. We know that they will grow up ... yes, they will grow up. With perseverance, and perhaps the patience of Job, one day we will stand with our teens on the mountain top and think ... "NO PROBLEM!"

When we do fail, we should thank God for *forgiveness.* For my family and me, forgiveness is an adventure—full of the risk and joy of saying "I'm sorry" or "I forgive you" to each other regardless of how hurt, wronged, or embarrassed we feel. We have found that our home and our family cannot function as it should without the daily practice of forgiveness.

Forgiveness is the ultimate means of encouraging the development of a strong family unit. If we are sorry for the mistakes we have made in our relationships with our children, we can ask them for forgiveness, receive it, and experience new strength and vitality in our relationship.

Throughout this book I've talked about the importance of setting goals that can help get us back on track when we lose our way, and keep us going when the going gets tough. I invite you now to restate and reaffirm the following goals as a reminder of the direction you want to take:

1. I accept the challenge of building a bridge of caring communication with my teen.
2. I will be sensitive to the developmental stresses of adolescence.
3. I will keep in mind how communication works and what to do when it doesn't.
4. I will earn the right to be heard.
5. I will exercise parental authority effectively because I know when and how to say no ... and yes.
6. I will listen in ways that motivate my teen to talk to me.
7. I will respond CALMLY to strong emotions.
8. I will work at resolving disagreements by following the conflict resolution model.
9. I will respond appropriately to my teenager's personality and temperament in our communications.
10. I will talk to my teen about his or her important life decisions.
11. I will confront my teenager's major problems directly and effectively.
12. I will make sure to communicate the five messages my teen wants to hear.

It's important to believe that you can succeed in reaching your goals—because the fear of failure often produces half-hearted, and ultimately unsuccessful attempts. Perhaps the greatest danger we face is our unconscious assumption that the family's communication patterns cannot be changed, that the future holds no promise for improvement. We must avoid such assumptions, because they can prevent us from pursuing the opportunities we have for positive change. The good news is that the past need not keep us from building a stronger family for the future—a supportive and happier family that can survive and thrive through all of the difficult moments of family life.

You may not yet have achieved these goals. Recommitting yourself to them will help build your determination to create the kind of family life that you want for yourself and your children.

NOTES

Chapter 1: A Parent's Toughest Challenge
1 Dorothy Sarnoff, *Make the Most of Your Best* (New York: Doubleday & Co., 1981), p. 4.

Chapter 2: What Makes Your Teenager Tick?
1 David Elkind, *All Grown Up and No Place to Go* (Reading, MA: Addison-Wesley Publishing Co., 1984), p. 99.
2 Erik H. Erikson, ed., *The Challenge of Youth* (New York: Doubleday & Co., Inc., 1965), p. 10.
3 Elkind, pp. 6-8.
4 Bruce Narramore, *Adolescence Is Not an Illness* (Old Tappan, NJ: Fleming H. Revell Co., 1980), p. 61.
5 Wizard of Id cartoon, by permission of Johnny Hart and Creators Syndicate, Inc.
6 Elkind, p. 69.
7 Dolores Curran, *Traits of a Healthy Family* (New York: Ballantine Books, 1983), p. 247.
8 Elkind, p. 9.
9 Robert Coles, "What Makes Children Grow up Good?" An interview conducted by Edward Wakin, *U.S. Catholic*, August 1979, p. 34.
10 Jay Kesler, *Too Big to Spank* (Ventura, CA: Regal Books, 1978), p. 83.
11 Norman Vincent Peale, "Runaway," *Guideposts* magazine, July 1978, p. 11.

Chapter 3: The Elements of Effective Communication
1 Albert Mehrabian, *Nonverbal Communication* (Chicago: Aldine Publishing Co., 1972).

Chapter 4: Five Keys to Communicating with Your Teenager
1 Ann McCarroll, "Getting to Know Children Requires Lots of Good Talk," Christian Science Monitor News Service. Reprinted in the *Denver Post*, June 19, 1980.
2 Norman Cousins, *Human Options* (New York: W. W. Norton and Company, 1981), p. 179.
3 "Cat's in the Cradle," words and music by Sandy and Harry Chapin. ©1974 by Story Songs, Ltd. All rights reserved. Used by permission.
4 Curran, pp. 40-41.
5 Lee Salk, quoted in Dolores Curran, p. 63.

Chapter 5: The Art of Saying "No"

1 Diana Baumrind, cited in Merton P. Strommen and A. Irene Strommen, *Five Cries of Parents* (San Francisco: Harper & Row, Publishers, 1985), pp. 87-91.
2 Strommen and Strommen, p. 88.
3 Elkind, p. 201.
4 Strommen and Strommen, p. 80.
5 Ibid., p. 91.
6 Ibid.
7 Ibid.
8 Narramore, p. 116.
9 Stephen Covey, *The 7 Habits of Highly Effective People* (New York: Fireside, Simon & Schuster, 1990), p. 91.

Chapter 6: Improving Your Listening Skills

1 Paul W. Swets, *The Art of Talking So That People Will Listen* (New York: Fireside, Simon & Schuster, 1992), p. 39.
2 Ann McCarroll, p. 39.

Chapter 7: Keeping Your Cool in Difficult Situations

1 Carol Tavris, *Anger: The Misunderstood Emotion* (New York: Touchstone, Simon & Schuster, Revised edition, 1989).
2 Lewis B. Smedes, *Forgive and Forget* (New York: Pocket Books, 1984), p. 12.
3 Peter Marshall, *The Prayers of Peter Marshall* (New York: McGraw-Hill Book Company, Inc. 1949).

Chapter 8: What to Do When You Disagree

1 Earl D. Wilson, *Try Being a Teenager* (Portland, OR: Multnomah Press, 1982), p. 51.
2 David Augsburger, *Caring Enough to Confront* (Ventura, CA: Regal Books, 1982), p. 11.

Chapter 9: Getting to Know Your Teenager Better

1 Dexter Yager and Ron Ball, *Everything I Know at the Top I Learned at the Bottom* (Wheaton, IL: Tyndale House Publishers, Inc., 1991), p. 95.

Chapter 10: Helping Your Teenager Make Important Decisions

1 Graham Greene, quoted in Ann Rosenfeld and Elizabeth Stark, "The Prime of Our Lives": *Psychology Today*, May 1987, p. 63.
2 Jerald G. Gachman, "Adolescence: An Eye on the Future," *Psychology Today*, July 1987, p. 54.
3 Venita Van Caspel, *Money Dynamics for the '80s* (Austin, TX: S & S Press, 1988), p. 51.

4   Alexander Austin and Kenneth Green, quoted in Paul Chance, "The One Who Has the Most Toys When He Dies, Wins," *Psychology Today*, May 1987, p. 54.

5   David G. Myers, *The Pursuit of Happiness* (New York: William Morrow and Company, Inc., 1992), p. 178.

6   Rich DeVos, *Compassionate Capitalism* (New York: Dutton, Penguin Books USA Inc., 1993), p. 10.

7   Harry Stack Sullivan, quoted in Charlie W. Shedd, ed., *You Are Somebody Special* (New York: McGraw-Hill Book Co., 1982), p. 102.

8   Neil Clark Warren, *Finding the Love of Your Life* (Colorado Springs, CO: Focus on the Family Publishing, 1992), p. 102.

9   Irene Kassorla, "You and the Person You May Marry," Charlie Shedd, ed., *You Are Somebody Special*, (New York: McGraw-Hill Book Co., 1982), p. 105.

10 Ann Landers, quoted in *Skills for Living* (Columbus, OH: A Project of the Quest National Center, 1982), p. 241.

11 See I Corinthians 6:18-20 and Exodus 20:14.

12 Allan Bloom, *The Closing of the American Mind* (New York: Simon & Schuster, 1987), p. 57.

13 Ibid.

14 Strommen and Strommen, pp. 129-158.

15 Ibid.

16 Ethel Leestma Swets, *Consecrated Hands* (Grand Rapids, MI: Zondervan Publishing House, 1956), p. 17.

Chapter 11: Responding to Major Problems

1   Elkind, p. 199.

2   David Elkind, *The Hurried Child: Growing up Too Fast Too Soon* (Reading, MA: Addison-Wesley Publishing Company, 1981), p. 88.

3   Peggy Mann, "How Shock Rock Harms Our Kids," *Reader's Digest*, July 1988, p. 101.

4   Ibid.

5   Ibid.

6   Quentin J. Schultze, *Winning Your Kids Back from the Media* (Downers Grove, IL: InterVarsity Press, 1994), p. 102.

7   Susan Baker, quoted in Peggy Mann, p. 104.

8   Fred M. Hechinger, "Saving Youth from Violence," *Carnegie Quarterly* (New York: Carnegie Corporation, Winter 1994), p. 2.

9   Ibid.

10 William J. Bennett, *The Index of Leading Cultural Indicators* (New York: Simon & Schuster, 1994), pp. 30, 31.

11 Ibid, p. 30.

12 William Raspberry, "TV's Violent Influence," *The Commercial Appeal*, February 4, 1994, p. 7A.

13 Ibid.

14 Hechinger, p. 7.

15 Dick Dutton and Brian Gleason, "It's Only Booze," *Church Herald*, March 1, 1985, p. 11.

16 *The Commercial Appeal*, February 1, 1994, p. A1.

17 William J. Bennett, *Schools Without Drugs* (Washington, D.C.: United States Department of Education), 1987, V.

18 Pearl Washington, "Family Ties Loosened by Addiction," *The Commercial Appeal*, April 28, 1986, p. C2.

19 Charles P. Hannaford, *Germantown News*, February 5, 1987, p.1.

20 *Time*, September 15, 1986, p. 61.

21 Stephen Arterburn & Jim Burns, *Drug-Proof Your Kids* (Colorado Springs, CO: Focus on the Family Publishing, 1989), pp. 183-186.

22 Harold M. Voth, *How to Get Your Child off Marijuana*, Patient Care Publications, 1980.

23 Louis Harris Poll, interviews with one thousand teenagers aged twelve through seventeen during September-October 1986, reported in *Children & Teens Today*, April 1987, p. 1.

24 David Van Bieme, "What's Gone Wrong with Teen Sex," *People*, April 13, 1987, p. 11.

25 Ann Landers, *Sex and the Teenager*, Creators Syndicate, Inc., 1987.

26 Bryan E. Robinson and Robert L. Barret, "Teenage Fathers," *Psychology Today*, December 1985, p. 70.

27 Josh McDowell and Dick Day, *Why Wait?* (San Bernadino,CA: Here's Life Publishers, Inc., 1987), p. 17.

28 Stephen Arterburn and Jim Burns, *When Love Is Not Enough* (Colorado Springs, CO: Focus on the Family Publishing, 1992), pp. 152-153.

29 Robinson and Barret, p. 69.

30 Sol Gordon, "What Kids Need to Know," *Psychology Today*, October 1986, p. 22.

31 McDowell and Day, p. 17.

32 Linda and Richard Eyre, *Teaching Your Children Values* (New York: Fireside, Simon & Schuster, 1993), p. 125.

33 William Raspberry, quoted in Barrett/Mosbacker, *Teen Pregnancy and School-Based Health Clinics* (Washington, D.C.: Family Research Council of America, Inc.).

34 Ted Koppel, *Time*, June 22, 1987, p. 69.

35 Richard Durfield, "A Promise with a Ring to It," *Focus on the Family* magazine, April 1990, pp. 2-4.

36 *The Commercial Appeal*, March 12, 1987, p. 2A.

37 William J. Bennett, *The Index of Leading Cultural Indicators* (New York, NY: Simon & Schuster, 1995), p. 78.

38 Ibid.

39 *The Commercial Appeal*, September 22, 1985, pp. B1-2.

40 *USA Today*, April 21, 1987, p. 5D.

41 Ibid.

42 Richard Krawiec, *USA Today*, March 20, 1987, p. 12A.

43 "Suicidal Failure," Suicide Tendencies, Frontier FLP 1011. You'll Be Sorry Music. Copyright ©1983 American Legion Music, quoted in

Tipper Gore, *Raising PG Kids in an X-Rated World* (Nashville, TN: Abingdon Press, 1987), p. 106.

44 "Suicide Solution," Ozzy Osbourne, Bob Daisky, Randy Rhodes. Jet Music Ltd. Copyright ©1981 Essex Music International Ltd. TRO-Essex Music International Inc. New York controls all USA and Canada publication rights. Quoted in Gore, p. 107.

45 AC/DC, "Let Me Put My Love into You" and "Shoot to Thrill," Black in Black, Atlantic SD 16018. Written by Angus Young, Malcolm Young, and Brian Johnson. Published by J. Albert and Son Publishing, Ltd./E. B. Marks Music. Quoted in Gore, p. 88.

46 Joseph Perkins, "Kids Too Often Play Victim," *The Commercial Appeal*, April 28, 1986.

47 Ibid.

48 *Newsweek*, June 6, 1994, p. 65.

49 Ibid.

50 Hechinger, p. 7

Chapter 12: The Five Messages Teens Want to Hear

1 Victor B. Cline, *How to Make Your Child a Winner* (New York: Walker and Company, 1980), p. 163.

2 William Glasser, *Reality Therapy* (New York: Harper & Row, Publishers, 1965).

Encouraging Words

1 Norman Cousins, *Human Options* (New York: W. W. Norton & Company, 1981), p. 68.

2 William Shakespeare, *King Lear*, I, iv.

RESOURCES

Resources for Parents

All Grown up and No Place to Go: Teenagers in Crisis, David Elkind, Addison-Wesley Publishing Co., 1981. Offers advice that will help parents guide their teenagers throughout the turbulent years of adolescence.

Boys! Shaping Ordinary Boys into Extraordinary Men, William Beausay, II, Thomas Nelson Publishers, 1994. Practical and inspiring suggestions for raising your preadolescent son to be a true winner.

Bringing out the Best in People, Alan Loy McGinnis, Augsburg Publishing House, 1985. Thoughts on how to help others excel.

Children at Risk, James Dobson and Gary L. Bauer, Word Publishing, 1990. Invaluable ideas and suggestions for countering society's negative influences and reclaiming timeless values.

Five Cries of Parents, Merton P. Strommen and A. Irene Strommen, Harper & Row Publishers, 1985. A perceptive study on what troubles parents most about raising children.

How to Really Love Your Teenager, Ross Campbell, Victor Books, 1993. How parents can let teens know they are loved and accepted.

Keep the Fire Glowing, Pat and Jill Williams, Fleming H. Revell Co., 1986. Advice on building warmth and cohesiveness in the family.

Parenting Isn't for Cowards, James Dobson, Word Publishing, 1987. Dr. Dobson's eleventh book reveals his insights gleaned from a survey of thirty-five thousand parents about raising strong-willed and compliant youth.

Parents of Teenagers magazine (308 Hitt Street, Mt. Morris, IL 61054-0545). A practical magazine with advice on how to build better relationships with teenagers.

Prodigals and Those Who Love Them, Ruth Bell Graham, Word Books, 1991. An encouraging treatment of how to respond to children who may have strayed down the wrong path.

Raising PG Kids in an X-Rated Society, Tipper Gore, Abingdon Press, 1987. Explicit review of the irresponsible excesses in the entertainment industry and steps parents can take to fight back.

Raising Positive Kids in a Negative World, Zig Ziglar, Thomas Nelson Publishers, 1985. Offers a positive perspective on how to raise children in difficult circumstances.

Rising to the Challenge, Video. Can be ordered from: Parents Music Resource Center, 1500 Arlington Blvd., Arlington, VA 22209. A video for parents describing in graphic detail certain rock music groups.

Single-Parent Family magazine, Focus on the Family Publishing (Colorado Springs, CO 80995). Equips single parents to do the best job they can of creating a healthy home life for themselves and their children.

Single Parenting, Robert G. Barnes, Tyndale House Publishers Inc, 1985. Advice on how to survive loneliness, anger, and rejections, and restore family relationships.

Six Secrets of Strong Families, Nick Stinnett and John Defrain, Little Brown & Co., 1985. Research-based study of healthy families.

Teaching Your Children Values, Linda and Richard Eyre, Fireside, Simon & Schuster, 1993. A practical, month-by-month program of proven methods for teaching values to kids of all ages.

The Art of Talking So That People Will Listen: Getting through to Family, Friends & Business Associates, Paul W. Swets, Fireside, Simon & Schuster, 1992. An encouraging guide for establishing positive communication patterns.

The Pursuit of Happiness, David G. Myers, William Morrow and Company, 1992. A well-researched study of the characteristics of happy people.

The 7 Habits of Highly Successful People, Stephen R. Covey, Simon & Schuster, 1989. Dr. Covey's work provides excellent tools for building relationships within families—between parents and teens.

When Love Is Not Enough: Parenting through Tough Times, Stephen Arterburn and Jim Burns, Focus on the Family Publishing, 1992. Guidelines for building a strong family and breaking the chains of past family dysfunctions—eating disorders, runaways, substance abuse, sexual abuse, suicide, and AIDS.

Why Johnny Can't Tell Right from Wrong—And What to Do about It, William Kilpatrick, Touchstone, Simon & Schuster, 1993. How to provide our young people with the stories, models, and inspiration needed to lead good lives.

Winning Your Kids Back from the Media, Quentin J. Schultze, InterVarsity Press, 1994. Stories and strategies for making the media your family's servant rather than its master.

Resources for Teenagers

Aim High, Dave Johnson, Zondervan, 1994. The Olympic decathlete made famous by Reebok's "Dave vs. Dan" commercials tells his story of moving from tragedy to triumph.

Alive, Tyndale, Campus Life books. An excellent daily devotional for teens.

Best Friends, 2000 N Street, N.W., Suite 201, Washington, D.C. 20036-2336. A self-respect and decision-making program for adolescent girls ages 10 through 15.

Campus Life magazine, Christianity Today, Inc. (465 Gundersen Drive, Carol Stream, IL 60189-9828). A bright and bold magazine for junior and senior high youth.

Creative Dating, Oliver Nelson, 1986. Ideas to inspire fun and fulfilling relationships.

Finding the Love of Your Life, Neil Clark Warren, Focus on the Family Publishing, 1992. Offers ten proven principles to help you choose the right person to marry.

Holy Sweat, Tim Hansel, Word Publishing, 1987. An invitation from the president of Summit Expedition, a nonprofit corporation providing adventure-based educational experiences for all ages, to learn what a peak performer does, why he does it, and how to make peak performance a lifestyle.

How to Find Your Mission in Life, Richard Bolles, Ten Speed Press, 1991. Available as a gift edition or as an appendix appearing in each annual revision of *What Color Is Your Parachute?* that helps the reader to develop a personal mission statement.

"Just Say No" International, 2101 Webster Street, Suite 1300, Oakland, CA 94612. A resource agency for kids 5-18 years old that can help them discover how they can make a positive difference in their schools and communities.

Man's Search for Meaning, Victor Frankl, Beacon Press, 1961. A psychiatrist's insights on the meaning of life after surviving concentration camps during World War II.

Mere Christianity, C. S. Lewis, Macmillan Publishing Company, 1952. A powerfully persuasive tour of thought leading to faith by a former skeptic.

Preparing for Adolescence, James Dobson, Tyndale House Publishers, Inc., 1992. Prepares the pre-adolescent to navigate successfully through the exciting new world adolescence.

The Book of Virtues, William J. Bennett, Simon & Schuster, 1993. Classic stories, poems, and essays that powerfully illustrate common virtues like self-discipline, compassion, responsibility, courage, and honesty.

What Color Is Your Parachute?, Richard Bolles, Ten Speed Press, current edition. An excellent manual for finding a job and choosing a career.

Who Needs God? Rabbi Harold Kushner, Pocket Books, 1989. An intriguing study of mankind's search for faith.

Referrals

Best Friends—202-822-9266
Bethany Christian Services Child Placement Agency—800-238-4269
Minrith/Meier New Life Clinics—800-NEW-LIFE
National Runaway Switchboard—800-621-4000
True Love Waits—800-LUV-WAIT

INDEX

Paul Swets—a husband, father, speaker, and pastor—has made a lifetime study of the art of communication. At the University of Michigan, he earned a Doctor of Arts degree in English, with primary research in the field of rhetoric, the study of effective communication. His first book, *The Art of Talking So That People Will Listen* (Fireside edition, Simon & Schuster, 1992) is now in its fifteenth printing. Dr. Swets has also developed a seminar for the parents of adolescents, How to Talk So Your Teen Will Listen, and co-authored a seminar for couples, Closeness Through Communication, with his wife. Information on both seminars is available from Concerned Communications (800-447-4332).

Judson Swets was elected president of his senior class and inducted into the Ridgeway High School Hall of Fame, an honor awarded to the top twenty seniors in his school who showed outstanding leadership and scholastic ability. He also lettered in cross-country and tennis. Jud developed a survey that provided original information for his chapter on "The Five Messages Teens Want to Hear." Eight hundred junior and senior high students from different parts of the country responded to his survey. Jud is a graduate of Wheaton College in Wheaton, Illinois, and plans to teach high school math and physics.